Middle of Nowhere

Middle of Nowhere

RELIGION, ART, AND POP CULTURE AT
SALVATION MOUNTAIN

Sara M. Patterson

UNIVERSITY OF NEW MEXICO PRESS • ALBUQUERQUE

© 2016 by the University of New Mexico Press
All rights reserved. Published 2016
Printed in the United States of America
21 20 19 18 17 16   1 2 3 4 5 6

LIBRARY OF CONGRESS CATALOGING-IN-PUBLICATION DATA
Patterson, Sara M., 1974–
Middle of nowhere : religion, art, and pop culture at Salvation Mountain /
Sara M. Patterson.
pages cm
Includes bibliographical references and index.
ISBN 978-0-8263-5630-7 (pbk. : alk. paper) — ISBN 978-0-8263-5631-4 (electronic)
1. Knight, Leonard, 1931–2014. 2. Outsider artists—United States—Biography. 3. Outsider
art—California—Salton Sea Area. 4. Installations (Art)—California—Salton Sea Area.
5. Christian art and symbolism. I. Title.
N6537.K618P38 2016
700.92—dc23
[B]
2015014396

Cover photo courtesy of the author.
Back cover photo *Salvation Mountain 002* courtesy of Joe Decruyenaer via
Wikimedia Commons.
Designed by Lila Sanchez
Composed in Minion Pro. Display type is Meridien.

For Leonard Knight, who taught the world to keep it simple.

And for my family—Carrie Lee Patterson, Evan Patterson, and Veronica Patterson—who taught me to appreciate all of life's wondrous complexities.

Contents

Illustrations

Acknowledgments

It was my father who first taught me to be a place-ist. At a family cabin in the Big Thompson Canyon, a cabin built by my great-great-grandparents, who passed it down to their daughter, my great-grandmother, my father told me stories that communicated the importance of that place to me. Through stories about the cabin, he told me that that place made us who we were. He showed me that the landscape itself was part of the constellation of symbols that made us a family.

Ever since then I've been fascinated by place and the way that it affects human communities and relationships. This is, no doubt, part of what drew me to Salvation Mountain and brought me back there again and again. It wasn't just the place, though. It was the community that surrounded the place and told its stories. For many visitors, Salvation Mountain has become one of the landscapes that makes their lives meaningful and part of the symbol system that makes them who they are. Salvation Mountain made Leonard Knight's life meaning-*full*, but it also touched and was touched by thousands of other hands. It was at Salvation Mountain that I was challenged once again to ask questions about place and the role it plays in human lives.

During my time at Salvation Mountain, I was helped by more people than I can name. Each time he saw me, Leonard Knight welcomed me into his home, as he did with every person who showed up at Salvation Mountain. Knight was confident that God had sent me to get the word out about Salvation Mountain, and freely shared his techniques, his life stories, and his time with me. For that, I am forever grateful. I am only sorry that he didn't live to see this book come out. I will never know what he imagined when he imagined my book, but I hope he would be glad about its arrival.

Other folks at Salvation Mountain were particularly helpful. Kevin Eubank, who died suddenly in 2011, allowed me to interview him, prepared meals for both Leonard and me, and helped me connect to other individuals who might assist me. Mike Phippen also enabled me to better understand Salvation Mountain and the community that surrounds it. Countless others allowed me to interview them at the mountain and/or sent me accounts of their experiences there. This book represents the accumulation of all of these helpful hands and shared stories.

As I worked on my manuscript, I was lucky to call Hanover College in Hanover, Indiana, my intellectual and communal home. At the library, Patricia Lawrence helped me order the necessary materials for my research and was a wonderful support along the way. The Faculty Development Committee financially supported research trips to Salvation Mountain. A scholarship support group was an important source of encouragement for me—thank you Jared Bates, Dominique Battles, Paul Battles, James Buckwalter-Arias, Krista E. Hughes, Mandy Wu, Xialong Wu, Mi Yung Yoon, and Fernanda Zullo. Dave Cassel, Mike Duffy, Veronica Patterson, Robyn Ryle, Kay Stokes, and Karla Van Zee generously read portions of the manuscript and offered important feedback. Departmental support for my writing came from Dave Cassel, Mike Duffy, Krista E. Hughes, and David Yeager. Finally, I appreciate the support offered by Steve Jobe as the dean of Academic Affairs.

My thanks go to the people at the University of New Mexico Press, particularly Clark Whitehorn and Karin Kaufman, for their help in preparing the text for publication.

I was also the beneficiary of so many lively and challenging conversations about my work. As a recipient of a Luce Fellowship from the Society for the Arts in Religious and Theological Studies (SARTS), I presented my research to group members who helped me think through several issues related to Salvation Mountain as a piece of religious art. Other conversations, particularly with Amy Hoyt, Kate Johnson, Sara Moslener, Jennifer Naccarelli, Quincy Newell, Katie Oxx, and Karla Van Zee, helped refine my thinking about several of the themes explored herein.

Without the support of my various communities throughout this process, I would never have finished this text. My friends Leticia Bajuyo,

Sharon Benton, Dave Cassel, Mike Duffy, Joyce Flanagan, Krista E. Hughes, Amir Hussain, Terry Jobe, Kate Johnson, Jamie Kepros, Mridula Mascarenhas, Jennifer Naccarelli, Quincy Newell, Zephirin Ryan, Robyn Ryle, David A. Sanchez, Nasrin Shahinpoor, Steve Steiner, Kay Stokes, Ruth Turner, and Karla Van Zee offered me important relationships and conversations throughout the process. Thank you. My teachers Janet Farrell Brodie, Robert Dawidoff, Jan Shipps, Ann Taves, Harold Van Broekhoven, and David O. Woodard intellectually contributed to this project in so many ways. That, along with their continued personal support, has meant so much to me.

Finally, my thanks go to my family, both biological and chosen. Your good cheer, thoughtful reflection, and laughter make me who I am.

Salvation Mountain art mailbox. Photo by author.

Introduction

It is a sculpture for the ages—profoundly strange and
beautifully accessible.

—SENATOR BARBARA BOXER

Tell me the landscape in which you live and I will tell you who you are.

—JOSÉ ORTEGA Y GASSETT

IT STANDS SEVERAL STORIES high. As you go up the yellow-brick road that winds up the side of the mountain—the path you are supposed to take because it is the safest—you can see that some of the paint is starting to slide. Leonard Knight spent over thirty years of his life painting this mountain, but its time in the desert sun with little upkeep has begun to show. Cracks are growing in the paint, and when they do, the infrequent desert rain gets in between the paint and the adobe mountain to which it clings. The paint starts to slip, like the foundation of a heavily made-up woman in a humid, rainy climate. Its face is falling. The paint buckles under the weight of people climbing. The cracks just continue to grow.

The desert doesn't help much. You would think that such a dry heat would preserve everything, raisin-like, like the faces of the people who live out here in the sun year round. But the desert has its own hidden destructive forces. Dirt devils rip through the region, kicking sand against the face of the mountain. The fine silt covers its base. With no one there to clean it, the dirt pools in all of the areas that used to be a gleaming white.

It's not just the sight of the mountain that indicates that it is falling apart. It's the silence. It's not like you would notice that silence if you hadn't been here before. After all, the desert is often a place people go to hear their thoughts. It is a space of silences. And yet this space was once full of sounds. Not the sounds of the modern world—of iPods blaring, of cell phones ringing or pinging with the next text message, of people shouting at one another to be heard over the noise of cars and sirens and the hullabaloo of life. It was filled with the sounds of storytelling, of people sharing their lives with one another by sharing their stories. It often began with Leonard Knight's story of how he came to live in this place and of how he came to decide to build a mountain in it. But that story was always followed by an exchange about how visitors also came to this place. About who they were out in the "real world." Where they were from. What they thought was important. Those types of exchanges don't happen so much anymore.

Other sensory experiences of the place seem dulled too. There isn't a smell of paint because no one has dedicated consistent time to painting the mountain in months. This place now smells like anywhere else in the desert. People still touch and are touched by the mountain, but they don't have all of the cues that used to help them make sense of the place, especially the stories that helped them know how to *feel* it.

After all, the artist who tended to it for thirty years, who dedicated his life to it, isn't there. A few years ago, his heart, eyes, and hearing failing, he entered a nursing home. There didn't seem to be any other option. The man he left to tend the place, Kevin Eubank, died suddenly. Although no health concerns seemed imminent, Eubank had a heart attack in his sleep. Then the artist, realizing his health would never improve enough for him to return to the mountain, gave up. He told a friend that there wasn't anything left for him to do to "help the mountain or the message." He wondered if he might be able to "do something from the other side." After that, he chose to go "off his feed" and quickly entered hospice care.[1]

He did not really want to go on in a world that was not *his world*. He died
on February 10, 2014.

There isn't anyone at Salvation Mountain to tend to the space in a way
that a sacred space needs tending. There is no one there to tell its stories.
And so the desert attempts to reclaim it, to return it to its previous existence. The desert is trying to make the place part of the space. It's not
that no one comes but that the people who do come tend to amble about
aimlessly, not knowing which path to follow or where they are "allowed"
to go. They need a guide.

The place itself is not dead. But it is, well, disintegrating.

LEONARD KNIGHT AND HIS MOUNTAIN

So who was this man who built a mountain in the middle-of-nowhere
desert? Leonard Knight was born in Vermont on November 1, 1931. He
grew up with five brothers and sisters in a farmhouse not far from
Burlington. Knight remembered the farm having "a couple acres of vegetables, three or four cows, a couple pigs. We had to milk the cows, had
to water three or four cows every day, take 'em out to pasture." When he
got all his farmwork done, Knight would sneak off to go see Western
movies at the theater. He loved their portrayal of the romance of the
American West, and early on he came to believe that California offered
all of the sunshine and freedom one could possibly want. But the freedom he imagined in the American West made the bad news that he had
to stay in Vermont and go to school all the more painful.

Knight did not enjoy his schooling and dropped out after the tenth
grade in order to work as a car mechanic. He did this until he was drafted
into the military in 1951 and sent to Korea. Later in his life, Knight con-
fessed that he wished he had had more courage at that point to fight the
draft. Even then, he wanted no part in killing anyone. One reason Knight
celebrated the new generation was that he saw in it the hope of a different
future. He always said he wished he had their kind of courage to fight for
peace and not war. He was sure that they would not allow a draft, that
they would not fight against and kill their fellow human beings no matter what the stakes. Even though he regretted his participation in a

military action he did not agree with, one that he did not believe he could reconcile with God's love for everyone, Knight had a fondness for people who served in the military and enjoyed it when active-duty soldiers and veterans visited him at the mountain. This special connection led the Patriot Guard Riders, a group of volunteer veterans on motorcycles, to accompany his cremains to two memorial services after his death (one at Fort Rosencrans National Cemetery in San Diego and the other at Salvation Mountain). Several of the members of the guard had known Knight and visited him frequently at the mountain.

When Knight returned from the Korean War, he bounced from odd job to odd job, including car salesman, car painter, and firefighter. It was a period in his life when he felt as though he had been running from something and was looking for answers though he could not even pinpoint the questions. He felt caught up in the "rat race," always finding that he never quite measured up to his culture's ideas about success. And yet, at the same time, he was never quite sure he bought what the culture told him a successful life looked like.

It was during a 1967 trip to visit his sister in Lemon Grove, California, that Knight had the conversion experience that transformed his life and gave him a new understanding of self and success. According to Knight, his sister, who was a member of an evangelical church, pestered him to go to church and repent. As with many brother-sister pairs, Knight felt this sisterly encouragement to go to church was both bossy and annoying. Knight tried to avoid her "because she made me go to church and I didn't like God then." And yet the nagging sometimes worked. Knight would head to church to appease his sister and get her to leave him alone for a while.

As he was driving home one day, Knight chose to listen to the advice a preacher had given him and began to ponder all of his sins. In the process of enumerating them, he was overwhelmed by how much they weighed him down, so he "stopped [his] truck on the highway in Lemon Grove, California, and all of the sudden . . . said 'Jesus, I'm a sinner. Please come into my heart.'"[2] Knight repeated the prayer over and over as he began to weep, feeling as though a new spirit had entered his body and a great weight had been lifted off of his shoulders. In that moment, experienced in a fully embodied way, Knight became a born-again Christian and decided to commit himself to Jesus. He immediately wanted to thank God for the gift of love he had been given.

After his conversion, Knight continued to work odd jobs, but he did so with a new sense of religious purpose in his life. The jobs served to pay the bills but were no longer the source of identity or meaning for him. Instead, his Christian identity became who he was and gave him a feeling of purpose. In 1971 that purpose was channeled into one project. That year Knight observed several hot-air balloons flying over Vermont. He noted the fascination that children had with the balloons: "'Daddy, what does that balloon say?' 'Momma, what's that balloon say?' And it didn't say 'God is love' on it. It said Budweiser or Coors. [So he] started nagging God for [one]."[3] What Knight nagged God for was his own hot-air balloon, one that could proclaim to those same small children a message of universal divine love. As he nagged, he began to collect various materials to construct his balloon. Knight even went so far as to visit Raven Balloon Industry in South Dakota, hoping to purchase a hot-air balloon for the $700 he had in his pocket, all the money he had in the world. He recalled that "it was like trying to buy a brand new Cadillac for seven hundred dollars, and they weren't interested. And as I was walking out I saw some big bags of balloon material and they said they sold them for five dollars a bag because it was material that'd been cut wrong. They might have a piece the size of a car, and one corner was cut wrong so they'd throw the whole thing away."[4] Knight quickly had a new plan to use those bits of material and create his own balloon. The balloon Knight constructed took over a decade to sew. He never used an industrial pattern but followed his instincts about size and shape. In the end, there was only one problem, and it was an insurmountable one. Knight "made it too big; it was two hundred foot high and one hundred foot wide, four times as big as the ones they ride in."[5] For his final of several attempts to fly the balloon, Knight journeyed to the desert outside San Diego in 1984. Once again, the balloon would not lift off and Knight realized that the material itself had begun to rot. Though he felt like a failure, he claimed that it was "not because of God. I felt like a failure because Leonard didn't listen properly. Leonard was too far ahead of God. Leonard wanted to do it his way."[6]

With his balloon lift-off seemingly a bust, Knight decided to show his appreciation to God in a different way. He promised God he would stay in that spot and build an eight-foot monument to God's love so that passersby would stop and ponder, just as he had done in his truck.[7] The "here" where Knight chose to stay is on the outskirts of what is today known as Slab City, California (a free recreational vehicle [RV] camp). The "slabs" of Slab City were left behind when the Department of Defense deemed the area, formerly a military base, unnecessary in 1961.

It was outside Slab City that Knight began his eight-foot monument, which eventually grew into a mountain as his time in the desert grew from weeks to months to years. After all, Knight did not have any "after" plans for once he flew his balloon. And so his time in the desert building a monument to God became its own satisfaction, success measured as the monument-turned-mountain grew and a new sense of calling and purpose developed. That first mountain was built out of cement, paint, and scraps he had found in nearby junkyards. Knight spent about five years working on his "God Is Love" mountain until, in 1989, a small rainstorm caused a crack.[8] That crack led to the collapse of the entire mountain: "Everybody thought I'd be discouraged, and people said—God must not want you to put that mountain up. But my thought was—Thank you, God, for taking the mountain down. Nobody got hurt. And, boy, I'd been telling everybody it was safe. And I just looked up and I said—'God, I'm gonna have to do it again. But I'm gonna have to do it with more smarts.'"[9]

Undeterred, and still finding fault in his own choices rather than concluding he had misunderstood his divine call, Knight rebuilt the mountain. This time he decided to "build it smart"; he used materials and techniques he had learned in the desert. Knight took straw bales, often donated by local farmers, and turned them into adobe bricks by mixing clay and water and adding it to the bales. He then shellacked over those bricks with gallons of paint. With additional "junk" that he collected in the desert—discarded tires, parts of cars, windows—Knight created the mountain that stands to this day. One of the significant architectural aspects of the mountain is the caves or "museum" off to the right. These caves are held up by pillars made of car and tractor tires stacked on top of one another. Once he had a stack tall enough, Knight would fill the center of the tires with an adobe mixture. The entire pillar might take anywhere from five to seven years to dry all the way through, but once it did, it could bear the weight of straw bales or anything else Knight wanted to use for the ceilings.

Salvation Mountain now reaches several stories high and is about one hundred yards wide. The mountain is covered in brightly colored paint, whatever colors pilgrims donate. The mountain has its own "yellow-brick road" allowing visitors to climb to its summit. Once at the top, visitors look out over waterfalls leading to an ocean scene complete with its own Noah's ark. In the distance and on a clear day, visitors can see for miles from the top of the mountain—the Salton Sea, the Chocolate Mountains, and the flatness of the desert floor.

Left: An unadorned tire stack filled with drying adobe. Photo by author.
Right: A completed tire-stack tree. Photo by author.

A DAY IN THE LIFE

Leonard Knight imagined the world in spatial rather than temporal terms. So to describe a day in his life would be to impose a bit of our own culture on him. For thirty years Knight measured time by the ebb and flow of visitors and the rising and setting of the sun. There was nowhere Knight had to be; he lived in his art home. Time did not matter to Knight the way it does to other people in his culture, who rely on calendars, appointments, and to-do lists. I first realized this about Knight when I interviewed him extensively about his life. I felt as though I was constantly asking, "And when did that happen?" And Knight was always responding either by saying, "I don't know" or by tying one of his life events to the size of the mountain or a new part of the mountain that he was building or painting at the time. For thirty years, the mountain measured time for Knight. Rather than a clock ticking away, Knight imagined instead a map of the world that flowed out from the space where he built a mountain out of gratitude for his own intense religious experience. He fashioned his own world where time and appointments did not matter at all. The only aspect of time that mattered to Knight he imagined in a spatial way. Knight cared about and thought most about the future and how God's love would permeate the world. These future events he saw radiating forth from the mountain and from believers who visited the mountain and went out to turn the world away from evil and toward love.

For decades Knight's days followed the same pattern. He woke early in the morning in order to complete some work before the day heated up and visitors started to arrive. In the last decade of his life, Knight's attention was focused on two primary activities. First, his goal was to repaint the surface of the mountain at least twice every year. This work ensured that that mountain was covered with a thick coat of paint, several inches thick in some places, and that any cracks could be addressed fairly quickly. His second task was to work on, build, and paint what he called the "museum," which is housed in the caves to the right side of the mountain. This portion of the site was Knight's work in progress for a decade and a half.

Above: Salvation Mountain's museum entrance. Photo by author.

Right: Inside Salvation Mountain's museum. Photo by author.

The Salvation Mountain museum room often described as Leonard Knight's "mantel."
Photo by author.

When he was at the mountain, Knight could be found on any given morning pouring five-gallon buckets of paint on the ground and "painting" it with a janitorial broom so that the walkways throughout the site were smooth and uncracked. The next morning he might be found pounding his fist into the center of a wet clump of adobe in order to make one of his world-famous flowers. The mountain was a never-ending project, and so Knight took on whatever task he felt like doing on any given day.

During the midst of all this activity, visitors arrived. "Hello! Make yourselves at home!" he shouted as they exited their cars—the greeting welcoming them to *his place*, his home. For visitors Knight stopped *whatever* he was doing to give a tour. One visitor recalled her encounter with Knight:

> I was kneeling in the dust to get a picture of a reclining chair inside what Mr. Knight refers to as The Museum, a structure made of bales of hay, discarded car doors, giant tree limbs, old tires, and adobe clay when I heard someone call a loud greeting from above my head. I was so startled that I nearly dropped my camera but I was delighted to find that the artist was home. . . . He climbed slowly down the ladder and extended a friendly hand. His skin was like a leather glove. He had a shock of white hair and the dark brown face of a serious desert dweller. His clothes were covered with paint and as casually as if we had already been in the middle of a conversation, he launched into the story of how he makes the adobe flowers that line the trunks of the trees. He told me how he starts with a big dollop of clay (he showed me the size with his hands) and how he just punches them, like this! He put his fist into the already dry indentation and I could imagine how much fun it is when it's wet.[10]

Knight's welcoming personality was disarming. He simply walked up to people and immediately treated them as though they were old friends picking up on a conversation they had already begun.

Visitors were the reason he created the mountain, and he would not even consider giving up the opportunity to interact with them, to tell them his story and his vision of a future full of love. He loved them, he said, because God loves them. Even though he loved these visitors,

Knight was also a hermit at heart: "I'm such a loner that it's almost embarrassing. I don't know how to explain that really. I love people . . . [but] I hardly know anybody's last name. I love to smile at them and thank them for paint and thank them for a paintbrush, and I really love them and they love me. But when I get too close to people, they always want me to do it their way. And then it looks like I want to do it my way. And most of the times, their way is right. But I still like to do it my way. I'm gonna make lots of mistakes, but let me make them."[11] Knight took his cues from his God. He was able to love everyone precisely because he thought God did, but that did not mean he had intimate relationships with everyone. In fact, quite the opposite was true. Knight rarely had intimate, two-way relationships with people. He was a guarded man who cherished his freedom and believed that in order to protect that freedom, he couldn't allow many people to get close to him.

Leonard Knight. Photo by author.

Yet when people visited Salvation Mountain, what they felt was that universal welcome to which Knight was committed. When people visited the mountain, they felt close to Knight. They were entering his world and his stories in a profound way the moment they stepped out of their cars. During a tour, an enthusiastic Knight guided visitors over to the right side of the mountain to the museum. After showing them the museum in progress and explaining the development of the mountain, an aging Knight instructed visitors to head up the yellow-brick road, the path to the top of the mountain, to take as many pictures as they wanted, and then to meet him at the base when they were all done. As visitors climbed and took pictures, Knight sat patiently in back of an old, broken-down, colorfully painted station wagon. Underneath a handmade shaded shelter, Knight waited for visitors to come up and tell their own stories of their experience of the mountain. It was there that he would give them postcards, magnets, and puzzles so they could take something home with them and share it with their friends. One afternoon in June 2011, I sat with Knight under the shaded station wagon living room and listened as a ninety-two-year-old World War II veteran talked about his time in California and how important his family was to him, especially after spending part of the war in a German prisoner-of-war camp. He saw in Knight a man who had left family and home to live in the desert, a kindred spirit. This feeling of shared experience stemmed not only from the fact that both men fought for the United States in wars abroad but also from the sense that Knight shared his values of family and home. It was his warmth and spirit that drew people to Knight—he understood them, they thought, even when he did not have a shared set of experiences. Knight made people feel—even the folks who came to visit the "crazy man's mountain"—that they were *at home*. It was the fact that he warmly invited them into his home that often allowed them to imagine a shared vision of the world.

During the afternoon—the hottest part of the day—Knight would curl up on an old sleeping bag on the floor of one of the caves. Because they are shaded, the caves are often ten to fifteen degrees cooler than the outside temperature. At that same time of the day during the hot summer, Knight might also head to the local canal, where to this day people can and do swim for free. This was an opportunity to jump into some cooler water and to bathe. The final place Knight might have been found on those hot afternoons was heading to the town of Niland in order to drink iced tea in a local restaurant, waiting for the sun to begin to set. Knight was well known among the locals precisely because he would travel in one of his art cars and wave to folks as he passed them on the street.

After an afternoon in one of these cooler locations, Knight headed back to the mountain to meet with anybody who came in the late afternoon and finish up any projects that he had begun in the morning. He was reluctant to leave the mountain, so he scheduled his days around visitors first and around getting work done second. In the evening Knight might continue to host visitors, swapping stories, playing the guitar, and laughing into the night. Knight loved to play the guitar and loved to sing. In fact, he recalled a time that he realized that he was "talking too much Johnny Cash and not enough Jesus" and committed himself to using his guitar and his song writing to help share the same messages that he offered in the mountain. Once his visitors departed, Knight retired to his home-within-his-home, a broken-down art truck located directly at the base of the mountain.

He carried on this pattern for decades. He did not travel much—his movement through space was limited to local trips—because he did not want to leave the mountain unattended. If a visitor dropped by, Knight wanted to be there. As Knight's health began to decline, his movement became even more restricted. His cataracts forced him to give up driving. Initially, his heart failure meant that he could not stay at the mountain all day long. Then those same medical concerns caused a decline to the point that Knight entered a nursing home, where he hoped to get well enough to return to his mountain home. Though there were several trips from the nursing home to the mountain, his dream of returning permanently to his home, where the world made sense to him, was never realized.

VISITING THE MOUNTAIN

I first heard about Salvation Mountain in the same way most people do, from someone who had been there and was excited about it. Two students enrolled in my Jesus in American Popular Culture course decided to visit the mountain as an example of a contemporary understanding of Jesus in American culture. The two twenty-year-old art majors road-tripped out to the mountain from Los Angeles and spent a weekend with Knight and other visitors to the mountain. They returned buzzing with all that they had seen and brought back a postcard to share with me. I kept that postcard on my refrigerator among to-do lists and pictures of friends and family. The image of the place stuck with me. After seeing the postcard, I knew I would visit the place, I just didn't know when. Like so many works of outsider art, images of Salvation Mountain invite people to it. The image makes us wonder how something like Salvation Mountain came into being. Scholar Timothy Beal in his study of roadside religious art describes the sentiment this way: "Who has the chutzpah in this day and age to do something like *that* on the side of the road? And *why*? What drives such a person? What desires? What visions? . . . In other words, you want to understand. You want to know, *What's the story?*"[12]

When I found out that an annual meeting of religion scholars would be held in San Diego, I knew I had a chance to learn more about Knight and his mountain. I invited a friend of mine along, wanting to see and talk about the place with someone else who studied American religions. We headed east out of San Diego and fairly quickly got lost, almost crossing over the border into Mexico at one point. We reached Salvation Mountain much later than we had planned and hopped out of the car. There was an eerie silence there. I'll never know where Leonard Knight was that day, but we must have arrived at one of those odd moments when he left the mountain to venture into town. My friend and I moved quietly around the site, wondering if someone might pop out at any moment to startle us. We went part way into the caves and then decided that we didn't want to go any farther. As we were heading out, my friend said, "This is my worst nightmare. It's a strange combination of Disneyland and evangelicalism . . . evangelicalism on acid."

I went home, glad that I had seen the mountain that had lurked in my thoughts and on my fridge for some time. I continued to think about it; I wasn't done with it yet. I still didn't know its story. In the meantime, I got a job in Indiana, offering new challenges to someone who studies religion in the American West. I returned to Salvation Mountain a year later to

interview Leonard Knight, spending about a week there. We would officially interview for an hour or two a day and then he would show me the
various projects he had under way. We would stop our discussions when-
ever visitors arrived. Knight always dropped everything for his visitors. I
started talking to those visitors too, and I realized that Leonard Knight
was only part of the story. His stories and his prophetic speech needed an
audience, and I wanted to know who the people were who made up that
audience.

It was in this way—moving from his account of his life to watching
him work on and explain an aspect of the mountain to seeing him interact with visitors—that I began to know Leonard Knight and to see that
this man who always told visitors to "keep it simple" was actually quite
complex. I saw how he interacted with people from all walks of life and
from all around the world to hear his message that "God is love." I saw
how many people left the place feeling profoundly moved by their experiences there. I realized that Knight and his mountain had a community
around them and that that community played a crucial role in the survival of the site. Knight was its caretaker, but visitors to the mountain
cared for Knight and provided him with relationships that made his
world meaningful.

I returned to Salvation Mountain five more times and stayed one or
two weeks each time. I talked with Knight, learning about his recent projects, and talked to visitors. Academic calendars don't line up well with
weather patterns in the desert, so I always ended up at Salvation Mountain
during the hottest times of the year, when, on a typical day, thirty to forty
visitors might arrive. Because Knight thought that God had sent me to get
the word out about the mountain, he was always comfortable with me
spending time with him and speaking with visitors. I would only speak to
them on their way out, after they had completed their visits. Some of them
answered written questions, some spoke with me at great length about
their experiences, and some e-mailed me their stories after they went
home. Kevin Eubank, a social worker who cared for Knight, once posted
on Salvation Mountain's Facebook page a request that people send me
accounts of their visits to Salvation Mountain, and I was able to gather
some stories that way. Through these different processes, I compiled the

stories and began to piece together the makeup of the community that surrounded Leonard Knight. Without his audience, Knight would have been a lone voice crying in the wilderness. He would have been a crazy man in the desert rather than a prophet and an artist.

I spent many hours sitting in the desert in temperatures of about 110 degrees, wondering what might pull people to this site. I heard many stories about why people came and why they returned again and again. Many reasons echo throughout the accounts. One of the most prominent is that Knight and his mountain seem to stand outside many worlds. People are drawn to the mountain because it defies easy classification and challenges some of our most basic cultural assumptions.

Sacred and profane, natural and unnatural, word and image, and belief and action are dualisms intellectuals may impose on the world that do not easily play out in people's lived religious experiences. Salvation Mountain reminds us that religion happens in bodies and in the material world. It happens as people come together to form communities and tell stories; Salvation Mountain reminds us that religion is not an individual but a communal matter, even when we are alone.[13] It may well be that the merging of these seeming contradictions heightens the appeal of Salvation Mountain.

As I compiled the stories, it was clear that the materiality of Salvation Mountain could not be sidelined or ignored; it must remain central to any analysis of it. Salvation Mountain is the desert. It is the work of a man who believed his hands were guided by God. It is a place that people do not just see, but climb, touch, and experience. It is material religion. In a culture that often touts itself as having banned religion from the public sphere, however true or false that claim may be, Leonard Knight had the foolhardy gall to build a private expression of his most intense religious experience on land owned by the State of California.[14] Knight burst through all of these cultural dualisms and created a mountain that *is* his belief. He built a mountain that expressed his religion for all the world to see, and he invited people to see it and to experience that religion for themselves. And he could only pull it off in the middle-of-nowhere desert.

In the middle of nowhere, Knight created for them and with them a sacred space that could embody their expectations for the future. As we will see, sacred spaces are worlds that must be maintained and storied. Sacred spaces, especially those offering a distinct and alternative world view, are fragile worlds, and the question of whether Salvation Mountain will survive Knight's death, and how, highlights this fragility. Perhaps we are witnessing the disintegration of a sacred space, or perhaps we are witnessing a redeployment of that same space for new visionary worlds; the only guarantee is that it will not remain the same. Whatever happens at Salvation Mountain, an exploration of the creation of that sacred space and the changes that have taken place since Knight's death will offer us unique insights into the intersections of art, religion, and place.

Knight's art truck at Salvation Mountain. Photo by author.

View of the back of the museum from the top of Salvation Mountain. Photo by author.

Art tractor at Salvation Mountain. Photo by author.

1

Outsiders All

Art, Religion, and Sacred Space

Some of us aren't meant to belong.
Some of us have to turn the world upside down and
shake the hell out of it until we make our own place in it.

—ELIZABETH LOWELL

EVEN THOUGH LEONARD KNIGHT'S religious conversion was profoundly shaped by the churches that he visited, and even though his born-again identity became central to who he was, during his time at Salvation Mountain, Knight refused to attend any church. For over three decades he did not go to church because he didn't want to "love Jesus secondhand."

This wasn't an easy choice. Knight's refusal hinged on his frustration with the separations he saw in Christianity. He believed that bigger churches lorded their numbers over other Christians, claiming, "I'm the biggest there is." Those churches, Knight thought, should be rebuked for excluding other people: "Hey, you be careful with God, because he loves everybody in the whole world. Everybody he ever made. Don't go around thinking things like that." Knight was concerned not only with big churches but also with the pastors who earned degrees and emphasized doctrine over the biblical text. "I don't care if it's the biggest church going, if they've got four master's degrees and they make a silo full of money every day. That is not interesting," Knight claimed. And he believed that those same church leaders picked on him "because I'm a dumb dropout from high school in the tenth grade."

Knight argued that church divisions were rooted in human debates that divided rather than united God's people. In the midst of the arguments about orthodoxy, he claimed that Jesus was left out. Instead he wanted "100% Jesus and God . . . 100%." Knight's view on the church as an institution was clear: "It's a complicated mess, if you want the truth. I wish somebody could put that in a nice way. Don't get so complicated. Keep it simple. God loves us all. Next question?"

When I first asked Knight if he called himself a Christian, he replied, "No, I call myself . . . I don't call [myself]. . . . There are ten thousand people out there calling themselves Christians and they are all fighting each other and biting and fighting and bickering. So I don't want to get mixed up in too many complicated things." Later, he explained that he was a Christian, but not like the Christians he had just described, the kind he believed populated the pews of churches around the world. He wanted to stand outside the church in order to call its bluff. He wanted to coax the church back to what he believed true Christianity was—gratitude for God's love. Knight saw corruption, an emphasis on material wealth, and orthodox doctrines as that which made things "too complicated." His keep-it-simple approach put him outside the church; he refused to attend even on Sunday mornings.

Much of Knight's life was spent as an outsider. While his Christian identity was key to who he was, he refused to associate himself with any group within the Christian community—to the extent that he hesitated to call himself a Christian because the term itself might conjure up in people's minds a different vision of the world than he imagined. At the same time that Knight purposefully stood outside the church walls, he also stood on the periphery of the art world that came to celebrate his work in the last decade or two of his life. Knight's life's work was a piece of art, and yet he never felt kinship with the art world. Indeed, he was flattered by critics suggesting that he was a notable artist but remained concerned that someone might think of him as an artist rather than a follower of Jesus.

It was a spatial move that truly unmoored Knight and allowed him the distance to both critique and embrace the church and the art world. That spatial distance fostered a sense of self in relationship to the Christian community and to the art world. Knight embraced his position as an outsider. At times that outsider identity was foisted on him by others and then embraced by him, and at other times he chose the outsider identity, exercising his freedom to decide who he would be in relationship to his culture. Knight's spatial distance allowed him to create a distinct outsider identity, one that later reinforced his standing in his community as a prophet and enhanced his ability to create sacred space.

OUTSIDER ART

Many call Knight's work "outsider art," a term used in the art world to designate the work of a broad category of untrained artists who do not follow the dictates set forth by educational institutions and museums. Basically, the term is applied by art scholars to those who haven't been trained as they (and the artists they know) are. In 1945 European artist Jean Dubuffet coined the term "Art Brut" (Raw Art) to "describe works created outside the art world and . . . interpreted . . . as rejecting the mainstream aesthetic." Believing that the term was "too French," British scholar Roger Cardinal employed the term "outsider art" in 1972 to describe artwork that stands outside the mainstream, embodies imagination, and explores "the psychic elsewhere." More recently in the United States, the term has been tied to the artist's identity, the aesthetic sensibility of the work, and the contexts and meaning of the artwork.[1]

In scholarly communities discussions of outsider art run even deeper. John Maizels, one of many scholars who study outsider art, expresses these sentiments when he describes it as "the extreme expressions of those outside society's influences . . . uniquely original creations that stem from the inner psyche. . . . They are . . . a compulsive flow of creative force that satiates some inner need."[2] According to such scholars, outsider artists manage to stand outside their cultures and are driven solely by internal influences. Journalist Greg Bottoms echoes these ideas by claiming that outsider art "is not fueled by aesthetic concerns, at least not primarily." Rather, he suggests, it is fueled by "passion, troubled psychology, extreme ideology, faith, despair, and the desperate need to be heard and seen that comes with cultural marginalization and mental unease."[3]

Several assumptions underlie these definitions. First, the very term "outsider art" implies something about how we understand taste and artwork. It exposes that we assume knowledge and education are strongly correlated to competence and talent: the more training and the more credentials, the more ability, we think. Outsider artists break through these expectations; they demonstrate that there is not a direct correlation between education and artistic endeavor or merit. They are noticed and discussed as being competent *without* being trained, and that becomes the defining trait of their artwork precisely because it goes against people's expectations.[4] In this discourse, outsider artists are portrayed as exceptions to the rules rather than challenges to the assumptions within the rules.

Understandings about outsider artists also expose our assumptions about what might drive the artists themselves. Art critics assume that untrained individuals must be driven by some sort of mental illness, religious passion, or some other set of "extreme" emotions. These suppositions are highly problematic. First, they define these artists as "other." Second, they suggest that trained artists are never driven by intense emotions, mental illnesses, or religious passion. Critics imply that these artists are outside of the norm, that they are not like "us." In these definitions, art becomes an antidote to some form of insanity that can serve the same function as "endless bottles of tranquilizers and psychotropic drugs."[5]

Though Knight's work has been included in several art collections of outsider art, those collections tend to pay little attention to the religious aspects of the work. Most works on outsider art seem uncomfortable with the topic of religion unless it is read as a cause of fanaticism and therefore a reason to "other" the artist. John Beardsley, who has described such religious art as "visionary art," explains that for religious artists, the artwork is linked to the experience of being born again and cannot be separated from its religious underpinnings.[6] Leonard Knight would agree; he knew that he was called an outsider artist and had mixed feelings about it: "A lot of people call it outsider art. They talk about that, but if they didn't talk about God almighty in there, I'd get sick."[7] Here Knight showed that religion was his primary motivation. Even so, we need not then conclude, as some art critics have, that his religious motivations were out of the ordinary or tied to some sort of psychosis. Rather, Knight was an artist driven by many complex motivations, both conscious and not, just as other artists are.

Because of his religious ideas and singular vision, Knight has been most frequently likened to two other artists. The first is Howard Finster, another artist driven by the desire to express his religious faith. Both men felt a divine call to create and both saw the attention to their artwork as evidence of divine support. Yet the primary difference between the two is that Knight (and those who knew him) never commercialized his endeavor. His art was never for sale, and he often claimed the ultimate ownership of the mountain lay in God's hands. In this way, Knight is very much like Simon Rodia, the second artist to whom he is often compared, who never sold his work but dedicated years of his life to his project. Rodia's Watts Towers in Los Angeles show a singularity of vision as well as sustained work on one piece of art.

The category of outsider art is itself problematic. It is a category too broad to connect its occupants except by suggesting that they are not the "us" of the art world. It is also a category that lumps together mental illness and religious passion, suggesting that the two are rooted in the same cause, neither one of which is normal. The category implies that the "us" of the art world are not motivated by these baser problems and passions but by some higher cause. The category creates class systems within the art world.

Knight's own experiences challenge these designations. He did not want to be remembered solely as an artist, with his religious calling sidelined. He wanted a both-and world. He was an artist and he was religious. His religion motivated him to create, most certainly, but that motivation transformed him from a wanderer to an artist with a home

The Watts Towers in Los Angeles. Photo courtesy of David A. Sanchez.

and a place in the world. It made him understand who he was. Leonard Knight's art made Leonard Knight, and Knight's art created a sacred space. Indeed, Knight existed outside of the highbrow art world. He never attempted to join that crowd. His distance from highbrow art was simply a result of the tastes defined by that world. Leonard Knight was an outsider and an artist, perhaps in that way he participated in the making of outsider art.

OUTSIDER RELIGION

It is only in today's society, in which a secular progress narrative has been widely embraced, that Salvation Mountain could be interpreted frequently without reference to its religious context and content. An understanding of Knight's theological underpinnings helps us to better understand his art, and we must engage that theology to truly explore his world. On the surface, Knight's theology seems quite simple, and it is to this simplicity that many pilgrims are drawn. His message was a universal one, standing in a long tradition of the American embrace of Arminianism—a theological position that argues that Jesus's death provided a universal salvation for all rather than an elect few, and that it is in the hands of the believer to accept or reject God's gift of salvation.

Even though Knight's theology was simple, it was not simplistic. We must turn to his artwork to better understand how his simple theology actually had many complex components. The largest letters on the mountain proclaim that "God Is Love." This statement, more than any other, encompasses the whole of Knight's theology. Knight described it this way: "I love everybody. . . . The major purpose of the whole thing is that God is giving his love to the world in a simple fashion. God loves everybody. It's just a simple, beautiful love story."[8] This sentiment is affirmed and expanded on the right side of the mountain with large letters announcing, "Love Is Universal." For Knight, God's love was universal yet also eminently personal. Knight believed that God loved people in their particularity and individuality. It was simultaneously a unique love and a universal love.

"God Is Love" on the face of Salvation Mountain. Photo by author.

According to Knight, God's universal love for humanity translated into the sacrifice of Jesus. In fact, Knight interpreted Jesus's outcry "My God, my God why have you forsaken me" (Mark 15:34 and Matthew 27:46) as evidence that "God couldn't look on Jesus because he was beat up so bad. . . . He went to the cross for me. Unbelievable that love out there and he did that for everybody."[9] Divine love manifested in the gift of salvation available to all people. The second-largest message on the face of the mountain is one that encourages pilgrims to say Knight's version of the sinner's prayer, the same prayer he said the day he became a born-again Christian: "Jesus I'm a Sinner Please Come Upon My Body, And Into My Heart." Knight's image of Jesus was one of a man knocking at the door of the heart of every human, waiting to be let in. He claimed that the sacrifice Jesus made was for everyone and that each individual, if willing to accept the offer and let Jesus in, could receive the promise of salvation and heavenly reward.

Since the day he became born again, Knight had imagined Jesus as

his closest friend. As he went about his work, Knight carried on a conversation with Jesus on a "one-to-one basis." "I get all alone and wow—
'Jesus I love you for yesterday. Hello God, I'm your friend.' Hours and all
alone. Most people really, to be honest, most people put Jesus off day
after day. . . . He's my friend, so I talk to him a lot."

Knight's "keep it simple" message maintained that this theology must
exist outside of any particular denomination. As stated earlier, he refused
to associate himself with any denomination or, for that matter, to attend
any church because, to his mind, this would have complicated the message. In this way, Knight made himself an outsider to all Christian institutions. He very intentionally stood outside in order to embrace what he
believed was God's universal message of love. On the whole, he believed
churches had gotten "too educated" and "too complicated." In the process, they had added layers and layers of doctrines and dogmas that
eventually muffled and distorted the simple message of God's love for
everyone. Knight indicated that all religious institutions, including those
in other faith traditions, have so corrupted God's inclusive love that they
no longer speak the truth. Knight's message of universal divine love, he
claimed, transcended the bounds of human institutions and denominations and reflected the reality of the divine—it was boundaryless.

Suggesting that the message transcended the boundaries of all the
world religions, Knight's was an inclusive Christian stance. If asked
whether one must believe in Jesus in order to have legitimate faith or to
participate in spreading God's love, Knight cagily responded, "Our only
job is to love everyone because God loved us first."[10] He accepted the
validity of other religious traditions and did not believe that people of
other traditions—Muslims, Hindus, Jews, and Buddhists—were going to
hell. In fact, Knight's theology of hell was relatively nonexistent, particularly in the last decade of his life. Knight was not concerned about people
receiving some ultimate judgment in the next life but was concerned
with developing and encouraging love in this one. This commitment
shaped his approach to other faiths. Knight embraced Jesus as *his way* of
finding God's love and transforming his life. In the end, though, his concern was that others were experiencing God's love and living that love in
the world; how they got there, their faith tradition, was less important.

Knight would certainly share his message about Jesus with those who wished to hear it, and with some who did not, but if they understood and felt love and God, he had no quarrel with them. He did not believe he was called to judge anyone. On this topic, Knight also intentionally stood outside of many Christian denominations that would claim that Jesus is the only path to salvation and that any other religious tradition will lead believers to hell: all peoples were included in Knight's vision of a peaceful and loving millennium. Visitors to the site that I encountered understood this about Knight as soon as they began to interact with him. His welcoming personality and interest in each person's particularity demonstrated his theological stance that his role was not to judge but to love.

Although Knight's message was universal, it had a particular flavor in the Christian tradition, a tradition that is not often linked with inclusive claims about other faith traditions. Like many Pentecostals, Knight's favorite biblical passages to quote were often from the book of Acts. Specifically, Acts 2:38 ("Then Peter said unto them, Repent, and be baptized every one of you in the name of Jesus Christ for the remission of sins, and ye shall receive the gift of the Holy Ghost.") and Acts 2:2–4 ("And suddenly there came a sound from heaven as of a rushing mighty wind, and it filled all the house where they were sitting. And there appeared unto them cloven tongues like as of fire, and it sat upon each of them. And they were all filled with the Holy Ghost, and began to speak with other tongues, as the Spirit gave them utterance.").

Knight took a literalist approach to these biblical texts and explained that he was simply repeating what the self-evident text itself said. And for him, it said that the Holy Spirit continues to work in the world, blessing believers with the gift of tongues as evidence of their future and blessed status. He would not admit to doing any biblical interpretation; in fact, he blamed many divisions within Christianity on intellectuals who attempted to "interpret" the text. For Knight, who preferred the King James Version, one should "go to the Bible and . . . see something exactly in the Bible, just leave it there." Knight's literalism, however, didn't confine him. Scholars of religion have often suggested that biblical literalists take a simplistic approach to the Bible that leads them into

"Jesus Fire" on Salvation Mountain. Photo by author.

what one scholar has called "an intellectual straightjacket." Yet literalism is not as restrictive as that image suggests. Many literalists cling to the historicity of the story but allow for immense creativity in thinking about the context and meaning of the stories.[11] Knight's mountain is one such example. Though he may have a literalist interpretation, the juxta-position of passages on the mountain shows a creative and spirited inter-pretation of the texts. Knight took the "Word" and made of it a material reality, one visitors could engage with all of their senses.

In this way, Knight truly embraced an embodied theology. Perhaps the two most significant aspects of this embodied theology come in his ver-sion of the sinner's prayer and his concept of baptism by fire. Knight's ver-sion of the sinner's prayer on the front of the mountain is rather distinct: "Jesus I'm a Sinner. *Please Come Upon My Body,* And Into My Heart."[12] When asked about the "come upon my body" part, Knight said, "I got that in there. In Revelation . . . Jesus stands at the door and he knocks to come in." When he described to pilgrims how Jesus knocks at the door of their hearts, Knight pounded his own chest, emphasizing the physical nature of the spiritual acceptance. He remembered attending a church before he moved to California, where he, along with others, were praying to have headaches taken away. It was only when he said the sinner's prayer that Knight said he felt his body change: "I started to repent. . . . I could feel it. . . . It felt so beautiful, like the sensation of God [it was the] sensation of a scripture that no other man had hardly seen it and we seen it. . . . And I haven't had a headache since."

Knight also discussed the Holy Spirit in an embodied way. At times he saw the spirit as a comforter (and for him "comforter" connoted a bed comforter). Citing John 14:26, John 15:26, and John 16:7, Knight explained that a "comforter is a quilt. You can feel a comforter. . . . And sometimes I feel comforted, because I ask for it." When Knight described this to me he grabbed a comforter off the floor of one of the caves and wrapped it tightly around himself, showing in a visible way just how close he believed the Holy Spirit could be and just how comforted he could feel by it. Knight admitted that the mountain did not mention the comforter because "God hasn't revealed it to [most churches] yet." Because Knight believed it was still a secret from most people, he did not share his ideas on the topic with many visitors. He was afraid they might not understand and, in the process, be driven away.

What aligned Knight with trends in the Pentecostal and Holiness traditions was not just his literalist interpretation of the Bible but also his focus on a second baptism by fire. For Knight this was a second embodied experience of his faith: "This happened to me the second day I got saved. Shi-ya-comma-mulk-you-lu. Oh-lay-babi-ock-tong-no-mi-calada. And I said, 'What's that?' I didn't know what it was, but it's in the Bible. Speaking in tongues is in the Bible. So God blessed me with his tongue."[13] Knight understood tongues to be a gift given to true believers since the time of the disciples. For him, the gift of tongues confirmed the truthfulness of the individual's born-again experience, but it was not a sign that a particular church was correct. Throughout his life, Knight kept up a private, frequent dialogue with God and so viewed speaking in tongues as a special prayer language that only God could understand.

Knight's theological choices were all rooted in an emphasis on religious experience and expression. This came through most clearly when he discussed his lack of education. Much as nineteenth-century Baptists and Methodists and twentieth-century Pentecostal and Holiness believers placed emphasis on *experience* over education as the site of religious authority, Knight often referred to himself as stupid and silly, thus reinforcing his own experiential authority. He claimed that "God scraped the bottom of the barrel to have me work on that mountain. Maybe he just wanted to prove that he could pick somebody that really couldn't do it and then make him do it."[14] In describing himself this way, Knight likened himself to other "little people" whom God had used to do great things. "I am just a puny little nothing," Knight said, "[but] all through the Bible in the Old Testament God used little people, a lot of times. . . . We got one more son out watching a few sheep, puny little David. Well, he turned into King David. So don't look at me like I'm a skinny little dumb thing if I'm quoting scriptures at you." In telling this part of his story, Knight repeated to visitors a core Pentecostal message: God and the Holy Spirit choose whom they choose. The message is ultimately a democratic one. The Holy Spirit may enter into and fill the body of anyone, and humans are not to judge that choice. In embracing this belief, Knight set the theological underpinnings for his social outlook. If humans are not to judge, if God loves everyone and the Holy Spirit may well show up in "the least of these," then he had no right to judge anyone or discriminate based on the racial, economic, and gender categories that society, not God, had created. Knight felt a religious call and command to love everyone.

Within American Christianity, Knight's theology and exegetical method are closely allied with the Pentecostal and Holiness traditions. At the same time, he attempted to universalize their messages in order to successfully share them with as many people as possible. In the end, Knight's mountain symbolizes many aspects of his faith. Most certainly, it carries the marks of the Scripture passages that were most significant to him. But the mountain also stands for Knight as evidence of what is yet to come. He was very certain of a postmillennial Second Coming of Christ, inaugurating a new reign of peace and love for all peoples. This view envisioned a world moving toward greater and greater amounts of love, which eventually would wipe out hatred, hunger, and war.

Because of this central belief, Knight disagreed with premillennialists, who suggest that the world will get much worse before it gets any better. Randall Balmer, a historian of American evangelicalism, describes premillennial dispensationalism this way: "Those who numbered themselves premillennialists believed that Jesus would return to earth to take his followers out of the world, an event known as the rapture. Those *left behind* would face hardship and judgment in a period known as tribulation. Eventually, however, Jesus and his followers would return to earth for the millennium, the one thousand years of righteous rule, before the culmination of time in the last judgment."[15] Premillennial dispensationalism profoundly shaped evangelical perspectives on the world. Christians were to view the world with distrust, seeing it as something against which they should define themselves. Whereas postmillennialists like Knight "held that Jesus would return to earth after the millennium, that there would be no disruption between this temporal age and the onset of the millennium," premillennialists believed that after a rapture the world would be marked by tribulations and trials.[16] Some premillennialists have read newspapers for signs that the end times are approaching. The future-looking orientation of premillennialists, their hope for a better world than the current one, provides an "eschatological goal" for human history. This view sees the present, and the evil in it that appears meaningless, as part of a divine plan for an Eden-like future.[17]

Knight argued with Christians who believed in such things as the rapture and a world full of trials and tribulations. He asserted that "the rapture is not in the Bible. . . . [It's] a manmade thing." Instead, "God is going to come down with a love. Everybody is going to love better. . . . And it's coming." For him, the future promised to continue to get better and better as the world chose to live into God's love rather than fight against it. While the mountain served as the promise of things yet to come, it was also evidence of movement toward that promise. For Knight and many of his visitors, the mountain is the message and evidence of the truth of the message all in one.

While Knight shared a lot with Pentecostals, he intentionally stood outside any institution. His unique insider-outsider stance allowed him to take on the role of a prophet. It might sound strange to refer to Knight as a prophet. Within the Judeo-Christian tradition, prophets such as Elijah, Jeremiah, and Isaiah rank as important men, and to compare these biblical prophets to anyone else may seem heretical. And yet Knight shared many characteristics with these people. The role of prophet occurs across cultures and is imagined by many cultures as a key role in human-divine relations. Prophets are intermediaries.

The definition of a prophet I find most helpful is a primarily sociological one, one that looks at the phenomenon of prophecy across cultures and focuses on the function of prophets in their cultures rather than solely on the content of their messages. Thomas W. Overholt's interesting comparison of Jewish prophets in the Hebrew Bible and Native American prophets is particularly helpful in showing the cross-cultural traits of prophecy. Overholt recognizes in these very different cultures that prophets have "some source of information or insight unavailable to the majority of the audience" and that members of the prophet's culture imagine her or him to have "some sort of direct contact with a deity."[18] He notes that there are two key aspects that give authority to the prophet in the mind of the audience. First, the "prophet makes the claim that the deity has authorized the proclamation of a certain message. The basis of this claim is usually a religious experience that is private and therefore essentially intangible and unverifiable by the members of the audience." In Knight's case this would be his born-again experience followed by the gift of tongues. Second, "prophets cannot be effective and cannot function as intermediaries unless the people acknowledge their claim to authority."[19] Pilgrims to Salvation Mountain offered Knight their witness; they authenticated his prophetic speech by finding it valuable and worth repeating. They gave him the authority of a prophet. Knight understood this to some degree; he knew that the mountain was the vehicle through which he had gained an audience: "For twenty years, before I came here, I'd go to a church and no one would ever let me speak any, because [I had] no education [and was] shy. . . . Then all of the sudden people wanted to listen to me." I asked Knight if he thought it was the mountain that made people want to listen to him and he responded, "Right, the mountain is it. . . . I feel very strongly, 'God Is Love' is popular. . . . I came here to put 'God Is Love' to the world."

Audience reception is a key strength to Overholt's definition of prophet. There are individuals throughout history who have claimed to have experiences of the divine and to speak for God. If there are no willing listeners, however, those individuals are quickly dismissed as heretics or lunatics. Prophets must have audiences: "The people choose their prophets; that is, they attribute authority to them because they perceive in the proclamation continuity with the cultural traditions sufficient to make what they say intelligible and at the same time innovations sufficient to offer the possibility of a new interpretation that will bring order out of what is perceived as chaos."[20] People choose their prophets based on the prophet's ability to speak to the problems of the time. Prophets call their communities to accountability and to action, suggesting that the *divine vision of how things ought to be* is very different from *the way things are.* As I will discuss throughout this text, Leonard Knight was a prophet to many people, people willing to travel thousands of miles to hear his message. That message, which some believe originates in the divine and some believe is just plain good, is one that challenges the cultural norms embraced by many in American society and around the world. Leonard Knight imagined a world quite different from the one in which we live.

This understanding of prophecy balances insiderhood and outsiderhood. Prophets arise in communities, and their speech is powerful precisely because they speak to what is going on in the community. Yet the prophet also claims a rhetorical distance from the community. In speaking about the will of the divine, in Knight's case, claiming to know what God wants, Knight was only able to critique the community because he rhetorically (and spatially, as we will see) distanced himself from it. He spoke of the way things ought to be—of another world where things would be different and everyone would feel loved.

For this reason, people were drawn to Knight and the wisdom he offered. Many called him a prophet, some called him a wise man. One man who visited the site understood Knight as someone who had achieved a level of enlightenment inaccessible to most others. Photographer Aaron Huey, who visited Salvation Mountain multiple times to photograph the landscape and its artist, said about Knight, "I have no doubt that what he did was the equivalent to sitting beneath the Bodhi tree or in Muhammad's cave, because I can tell you from my time with him that he was *awake*. And perfectly without doubt as to his purpose on this earth."[21] Huey too saw Knight as a man set apart who had an understanding of the workings of the universe that few others found during a lifetime. He saw Knight as a man who was truly alive.

OUTSIDER PLACES

Leonard Knight escaped to the desert, the land of revelations, in order to enter into a space where he had the freedom to create a world that gave him purpose and meaning. Salvation Mountain has many things in common with what religious studies scholar Timothy Beal has called "roadside religion": Knight's artwork came forth from an intense religious experience, his private and public lives were one, and his work is considered "far from normative" within the artistic and religious mainstreams.[22]

Yet Knight's work differs in at least one significant way. Even though his work is indeed on the side of a road, that road is not a main thoroughfare. In fact, Knight's mountain is really not on the way to anywhere else, unless one is headed to Slab City. That this is true is important for two reasons. First, the community that journeys to Salvation Mountain was and is an intentional community of people who have demonstrated some level of commitment to the place. Salvation Mountain is a destination. Second, that journey often creates not just a physical distance from civilization and its values but also an imaginative distance. One must journey to the world of Salvation Mountain with a physical movement through space as well as an imaginative movement—Salvation Mountain is an outsider place. It is the desert; it is the middle of nowhere.

Knight's life followed the pattern of early Christian desert ascetics, who escaped a society and church they found too materialistic, too complicated, and too corrupt, and fled to the desert to focus on their relationship with God. These desert hermits "did not reject society with proud contempt, as if they were superior to other[s]." Rather, they fled their social worlds because those worlds were "divided into those who were successful, and imposed their will on others, and those who had to give in and be imposed upon." These individuals wanted neither option; they went to the desert to avoid such social choices. Yet they were "eminently social," and the worlds they sought were those where everyone was "truly equal, where the only authority under God was the charismatic authority of wisdom, experience and love."[23] In the desert they were sought out by fellow believers who could not or chose not to leave their communities but believed the desert hermits had found a special type of wisdom alone in the desert—a type of wisdom they and everyone else needed. It was precisely because the desert hermits had renounced the values their society held dear that they were perceived as having a special and necessary type of wisdom. People came from great distances, even overseas, to hear the wisdom these desert inhabitants offered.[24]

Why is the desert the landscape to which so many of these ascetics are called? The lack of points of reference can easily lead to a sense of finitude in a vast sea of sameness. The desert is the starkest of landscapes, one where people might reach out to the divine for the basic necessities of survival. It is a landscape that forces us to reckon with our limitations. It is a landscape of scarcity. The desert is a place of emptiness, providing a glimpse of "unfathomable singularity." It is a place where one can experience solitude, and that solitude can shed light on what it means to be in community. For these reasons, the desert is "the environment of revelation."[25]

It is in the desert, in the midst of this disorientation, that Leonard Knight built his revelation, his landmark. In fact, he built on a long Judeo-Christian tradition of celebrating what happens in the desert. It was through the desert that Moses and the Israelites wandered, searching for their promised land. It was in the desert that they were taught their ultimate reliance on God for their manna and for their lives. It was in the desert that Jesus spent forty days and forty nights, learning that he needed God, his identity, and his ability to overcome evil with faith. Throughout the centuries the desert has offered believers a place to test their faith and their reliance on God for what they need. The desert has functioned as a place on the boundaries where trials must be overcome, often by sheer force of will and faith in God. The desert did the same for Leonard Knight.

It did what it did for hundreds of Christian monastics who went to the desert to withdraw from the world. They depicted the desert as "both a paradise, where people may live in harmony with wild animals, and at the same time a place of trial where ascetics encounter the inner and outer demons." For these Christians, the desert allowed them to live between two worlds—the material and the spiritual. As Philip Sheldrake explains, "To move to the desert was both a journey towards a holy place and away from the place of sin, metaphorically speaking. To strive to perfect oneself morally involved a topographical displacement."[26] When Knight went to the desert, he went through a process of being displaced and then creating place. It was here that he had the audacity to build a mountain, a point of reference and a site of reorientation, one he thought might orient people to the ultimate infinity of God.

In creating a mountain, Knight venerated another form that has long been celebrated in the Judeo-Christian traditions. In fact, he encountered God on a mount in the same way that many of the most celebrated prophets had: "The one god of the Hebrews held summits with Abraham on Mount Moriah, Moses on Mount Sinai, and Elijah on Mount Carmel. The New Testament—especially the Gospel of St. Matthew—contains numerous references to lofty sites. Satan took Jesus to an 'exceeding high mountain' to tempt him with an omniscient view of creation. On his own, Jesus went to the mountains to pray. It was from a mount that he preached the Beatitudes."[27] For these individuals and for numerous other biblical stories, mountains provide a meaningful and important backdrop—they are neither things to be climbed nor things to be feared but places where humans encounter God. Mountains serve as places of sanctuary for the persecuted and as places of retreat for leaders. Knight's mountain attempts to serve these same purposes, providing rest for the traveler and a place to encounter God.

Why are we drawn, as so many have been in the past, to the desert ascetics who flee society, leave behind all of its rules and expectations, and go out into the desert in order to experience something *more authentic*? Perhaps it is precisely this impulse, to find the authentic, that drives people to seek out the wisdom desert fathers and mothers have to offer. Their commitment to their ideals and values certainly seems exemplary—they are willing to sacrifice family and security in order to find experiences of the divine. In so doing, in becoming outsiders to the culture they wish to critique, these desert ascetics also create a moral high ground. It is from the scarcity of the desert that one can authentically critique all of the decadence of society. Desert ascetics also enable their followers to imagine another place, an outsider space, where the world operates differently. By spatially distancing themselves from society, by making themselves outsiders through miles of space, they are able to create a different world. Others travel between worlds to see the ascetics, to imagine something different, and to return home with new visions of how things ought to be.

At Salvation Mountain, Knight set up the world as he believed it ought to be. Many people may look at Salvation Mountain and wonder why anyone would choose to live his life in the middle of a desert, at some distance from the closest town, and with shade only from the artwork he has created. The answer to the question of why *this* place is a complicated one. Knight would tell you that he had nothing to do with it. He may have thought he did when he set off to California for the right place to launch his homemade hot-air balloon. But, claimed Knight, God had other plans: "God did all the thinking and the planning, and God put me in this place. And I believe that God guided my paintbrush an awful lot."[28] Knight also said that he had no intention of staying long in the desert after his hot-air balloon failed to fly for the last time. He planned to stay one week and build an eight-foot monument that proclaimed God's love: "Twenty-five years later I'm still here. . . . I found out the mountain is here, the clay is here, and I think God is telling me I'm going to stay longer."[29]

Knight's words suggest that he believed the mountain preceded his own arrival in the desert in some imaginative way. Yet it was only in the desert, away from the trappings of society, that he could set up an alternate world. As he told and retold his story, Knight communicated to his listeners a sense that the mountain they walked on was a sacred spot, set apart by the divine. A series of processes occur to designate the mountain as sacred space.[30] First, Knight's personal religious experience made the ground sacred for him. Even after experiencing multiple artistic failures out in the desert, Knight stayed in that location and eventually built his mountain there. "God guided me here," Knight recalled. "It wasn't my wanting to stay."[31] It was *in that place* that Knight's world and his place in it became meaningful for him. Until he moved to the desert in 1984, he had considered himself an average fellow, one who was blessed by Jesus's sacrificial death, but average no less. It was in the desert that Knight dedicated himself full time to building his artwork. Most important, though, for the site's sacred status were the stories Knight began to tell about it—of the sacrifice Jesus made for him, of the failed attempts he made to thank Jesus, of how he came to be in that place. In this way, the space became a setting and character in Knight's stories; in stories *this* place became *a place.*

And Knight, with the help of others, made this space a sacred space. Religion scholars David Chidester and Edward Linenthal argue that there are three primary views of sacred space in contemporary space studies. Each one recognizes that the fact that a site is considered sacred is due to situation, perspective, and context. No space is forever and always sacred; it is the human activities that happen in the space and the way a space is *seen* and *felt* that mark it as sacred. The authors argue that sacred spaces are (1) ritualized spaces, where humans undertake symbolic and repeated activities; (2) meaningful spaces, where humans create environments that bring order and meaning to their lives; and (3) contested spaces, not inherently meaningful, but sites where meaning and significance are always disputed.[32] Each of these is a component of Salvation Mountain's status as a sacred site. And yet perhaps the most important aspect of Salvation Mountain's status as a sacred site is that it must be maintained. If nothing else, the past several years at Salvation Mountain have proven that sacred spaces must be ever and always storied and maintained. Sacred space is tended space—it is space where people interact and tell stories with one another. It is space where people create worlds of meaning with one another. In the case of Salvation Mountain, it is space where a new and alternate vision of the world and its future was created through story and relationship. It is a space where Knight and his pilgrims oriented themselves in the world.

Although Knight's stories and artwork mark the sacred status of the space, its status was also reinforced daily through ritual.[33] Since Salvation Mountain became a popular destination for pilgrims of all types, the ritual act of pilgrimage buttressed Knight's claims that the space is somehow set apart. The embodied activities of participating in the artist's tour, listening to his stories, climbing the mountain to experience Knight's religious expression from multiple angles, and bringing gifts to a man many consider a prophet were all actions that affirmed Knight's designation of the site as special and sacred.

Knight developed a reputation with all types of pilgrims as a caring and charismatic dispenser of simple wisdom. Knight fled a world he thought was too materialistic and a church he believed had corrupted God's message by making it too complicated. Pilgrims often pinpoint Knight's simple message of God's universal love for all as precisely what is missing from society. In order for Knight to obtain this wisdom and develop spiritually, he had to *get away* from the culture he believed was corrupt. Knight escaped to the desert of California to a space that was uninhabited and seemingly unowned (the State of California did not claim an interest in the land for decades while Knight set up his camp). It was only in this space that was made sacred first by the narratives he told about it, second by the mountain he built on it, and finally by the rituals he enacted with pilgrims there that Knight was able to transgress boundaries in the way he did.

It was *away* from the culture that Knight could build a private, artistic expression of religious experience on public lands. It was *away* from the culture he found too materialistic, too focused on money, and too attached to a false notion of success that Knight was able to set up an alternative world with a distinct system of exchange. Knight's alternative system has at its base the notion of gift giving. His God gave him the gifts that enabled him to build a mountain; that mountain was then his gift to the world. Pilgrims proffered gifts in exchange for the wisdom Knight offered them—the wisdom he found in the sacred spaces of the California deserts—*away* from society. It was in this set-apart space that Knight fashioned his mountain to serve as an invitation to all peoples to participate in a peaceful and loving millennium. It was in this space that Knight became a prophet.

The relationship between sacred space and prophetic activity is important here. It was at a physical distance from the culture he lived in that Knight could create a rhetorical distance that allowed him to embrace a prophetic voice. He fashioned a prophetic platform from which he could operate as an insider-outsider, a voice crying in the wilderness with an audience who took the message home. By creating an alternate world through ritual, story, and artwork, Knight fashioned a platform from which he could critique the culture outside that world. On that prophetic platform, Knight spoke of a different world. Performing ritual acts that pointed to his vision of the future allowed both Knight and pilgrims to live a small piece of that future.

OUTSIDERS ALL

Timothy K. Beal suggests that works of outsider art may also be thought of as works of "outsider religion." In them he sees that "it is precisely in their marginality that they open avenues for exploring themes and issues that are central to American life."[34] Because Salvation Mountain stands at the intersection of outsider space, outsider art, and outsider religion, it can teach us about the intersections of place, religion, and art. Leonard Knight's Salvation Mountain is an outsider space; because it serves as a platform of a powerful critique of the culture and its categories, it opens the opportunity for profound experiences to those who journey to it.

Those profound experiences defy the neat categories we embrace in our culture. These categories are dualistic in nature, suggesting that the world is divided into either/or options and that within every dualism there is a hierarchy (for example, God/humanity, spirit/matter, belief/ action, and supernatural/natural are all common dualisms found within Christianity and the larger Western culture). In each dualism, the first option is privileged over the second, which is devalued. Knight's mountain challenges these dualisms and in so doing asks us to rethink them. His artwork collapses dualisms just as early Christians claimed that "the Word became flesh," suggesting that God entered into the material realm in profound ways. Knight created a material manifestation of his understandings of God, believing that God's love radiated outward from the mountain, embracing all who heard the message.

As we will see, the outsiderness of Salvation Mountain highlights the spatial and material aspects of religion. Scholars and practitioners of religion, particularly of Christianity, tend to focus on beliefs, suggesting that beliefs are the core of religious identity and that practices and rituals are secondary to faith. At the same time, we live in a culture that tends to privilege sight—*I have to see it to believe it*—over the other senses. Because Salvation Mountain bursts through dualisms the culture takes for granted and because it asks people to touch and to feel the materiality of its claims, it exposes the messiness of religious identity and shows us how religion does not fit into the neat categories that scholars and practitioners alike try to foist upon it. Salvation Mountain forces us to take all sensory experiences seriously and demands that we look not only at the experience of touching but also at the object being touched. In the words of religious studies scholar Brent Plate, "While it may seem I am doing the sensing and meaning making, the objects themselves are giving me input, speaking to me."[35] Plate's point is that as humans touch, they are not engaged in a solitary experience: the object being touched shapes our experience of it in profound ways. This argument echoes an argument made by Belden Lane about sacred spaces: "Personal identity is fixed for us by the feel of our own bodies, the naming of the places we occupy, and the environmental objects that beset our landscape." Lane further argues that the "place, in other words, demands its own integrity, its own participation in what it 'becomes,' its own voice. A sacred place is necessarily more than a construction of the human imagination alone."[36] Both Plate and Lane are emphasizing the relational nature of our sensory experiences.[37] We must not only think about who is doing the touching but also take into account what is being touched. Both humans and the landscape they occupy participate in making and maintaining sacred space. It is only in the study of the relationship between toucher and touched that we can better understand the religious experience. Salvation Mountain, because it invites visitors to engage all of their senses, troubles our attempts to create clean categories; it forces us to reckon with the messiness of relationality and its role in religious experience. The mountain requires us to consider the ways that space and matter lie at the heart of religious experience and identity.

The creation of sacred space at Salvation Mountain is key to this story and points to broader themes in religion and the American West. Knight went to California having watched Western films that promised him a place of real freedom. There he set up a religious world that had no real past; rather, it anticipated a future peaceful millennium that would expand outward from Salvation Mountain. That vision, though, has its costs. Knight's mountain is on the border of many worlds and is a contested space. The threat that it will be reclaimed because it is situated on government-owned land and the threat that it might be reclaimed by the harsh desert climes where he built it all point to issues that rise again and again around religions in the American West. In building his mountain in the West, Knight attempted to take ownership of the space for God while embracing the freedoms and promised utopian futures of the West. The pilgrims who followed him there often relished those same western dreams and hoped to enact their own western narratives. Together, Knight and his visitors attempted to create and actively work to maintain a place set apart.

Intentional outsider identities require constant maintenance, in part because there are no clean categories for identity and experience. As we will see in the next chapter, Salvation Mountain is a both-and world. It stands on the outskirts and therefore on the border, and in so doing it troubles our attempts to classify and categorize. While Knight intentionally embraced an outsider identity, we will see that such an identity was not always clear cut. He often operated on the borders, straddling categorical divisions while using them as platforms of critique. Salvation Mountain's outsiderhood relies on the ritual constructions of peoplehood and communal mapmaking that Knight and his pilgrims enacted. Knight and his visitors imagined a space on the periphery as a momentary center and claimed for themselves a message that challenged the values their culture held dear. In so doing, they imagined a different future, the world as they believed it *ought to be*.

"Nowhere Else Is Like This"

The Space of the Place

The Salton Sea looks good from afar, it really does. Water, it's pretty. But you go down there, forget it.

—MARY BELLARDO

ONE PARTICULARLY HOT AND slow afternoon at Salvation Mountain in the summer of 2010, I decided to get back in my air-conditioned car and head to Slab City, the RV park just down the road, to take pictures.[1] I drove through the sparsely populated town and looked around and then chose to head back behind the Slabs to photograph the canal. As I drove down the unmarked winding dirt roads, I had to make several choices where the roads forked. I continued on for a while and then felt as though I should turn around before I got lost. Not thinking anything about turning my car around in the middle of a dirt road in the desert, I simply stopped and began to turn. As soon as my car tires went slightly off the "road," they sank into the sand. In my attempts to get the car out, I ended up in a car with sand virtually up to its belly. Trying to move forward or backward only dug me in further. I was stuck.

There was no cell phone service, so I determined that the best thing to do would be to walk back toward Slab City and on to Salvation Mountain. I hoped I was going the right direction and that my sunscreen would hold out. I walked and wandered for about an hour before finding myself back in Slab City, where I asked a young boy to show me the route back to the front entrance of the town. We walked by angry barking dogs and a very wizened and sunburned old man who said, "A lady like you better get to where she's going before dark"—not the kind of thing I wanted to hear.

From the entrance, I walked back to Salvation Mountain, where I was able to call AAA services. But explaining my location was nearly impossible. Salvation Mountain and Slab City weren't on any maps. Luckily, the service found a driver who knew what I was talking about and was willing to drive along the dirt roads with me as I looked for my car. Up until that afternoon, I knew that place was important at Salvation Mountain, but I had not taken it seriously enough. I began to think of it in a new way. I had experienced the intense desert heat before, but I had always done so in close proximity to a car with air-conditioning and a cold drink of water. That afternoon I learned many lessons about the desert: how disorienting it can be in the sameness of its landscape, how quickly one can feel the effects of not having enough water, and how unbearable the sun can be without an inch of shade anywhere in sight. That afternoon and evening I also learned many lessons about the space surrounding the place. The desert is a landscape where one is reminded of how fragile human existence is. In the desert, it is undeniable that we are profoundly shaped by place. Leonard Knight understood that well. He knew that *place* made him who he was. And it was place that was so central to how Knight saw the world.

The first question Knight always asked people was "Where are you from?" Identifying people by tying them to *place* speaks volumes about Salvation Mountain. Names, occupations, and religious affiliations may have come up in conversation, but more often than not, they did not. Knight told pilgrims a story about how he migrated from Vermont to California, from place to place. That story of migration began to communicate the importance of place. In his religious journey from sinner to saved, Knight most understood his own salvation, his new status, out in the middle-of-nowhere desert. It was there he realized who he was. *Who* Knight was, was inextricably connected to *where* he was. In a profound way, the space was the man. It is for precisely this reason that an understanding of the geography of the Southern Californian desert—the space that surrounds the place—helps situate Leonard Knight and his mountain in their story. The landscape itself was a character in the creation of Leonard Knight just as much as Leonard Knight was a creator of the landscape.

The setting of Knight's artwork, the desert of Southern California, provides a stark contrast to the artwork itself. The desert is covered with little but sagebrush and a fine silt that can kick up into daily miniature tornadoes that zoom through the landscape, whipping up long columns of dirt in their wake. The blazing sunlight refracts from every particle, burning visitors' eyes if they stare for too long. Look away and the desert sky is bounded only by a level horizon: this infinite view offers a limitless and disorienting world, a world that feels freeing and terrifying all at the same time.

As one drives eastward from San Diego on Interstate 8, through California's Coast Ranges and down into the Imperial Valley, the landscape changes from lush beach city to rocky mountainous terrain to desert. Both Melchior Díaz (in the sixteenth century) and Don Juan Bautista de Anza (in the late eighteenth century), the first Spanish explorers to encounter the area, deemed the Colorado Desert too harsh and unkind to be habitable. Not surprising for a region that reaches 120 degrees in the summer months. It is a desert valley that few lived in for centuries, a place that was hardly noticed even in 1848, when the Treaty of Guadalupe Hidalgo, which ended the war between the United States and Mexico, drew a national border through it, making American what was once part of Mexico. This two-ness characterizes the region. As one drives eastward on I-8 and enters the Imperial Valley, one enters into a land of contradictions: of opportunity and failure, of built gardens and harsh desert, and of freedom and constraint. This land of contradictions is the space around the place. It is a place that lies at a nexus of American concerns, including immigration, military power, water issues, and saving wildlife hurt by the technologies of civilization. It is a place of both dreams and nightmares;

it is a place where Edenic visionary worlds and postapocalyptic dystopias confront one another. The contradictions contribute to Salvation Mountain, making it what it is and shaping both Leonard Knight and his pilgrims' experiences.

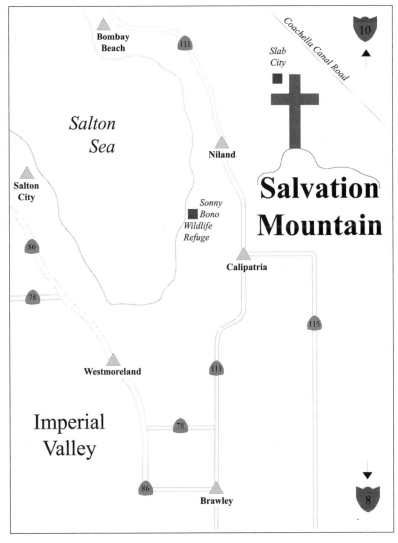

Map of the area surrounding Salvation Mountain. Courtesy of Evan Miller.

GARDEN AND DESERT

Salvation Mountain lies in the Imperial Valley between the Chocolate Mountains and the Salton Sea. The Salton Sea is one of the largest geographical features in the valley, a valley that was once appropriately called the Valley of the Dead because it had no lake, only an old, dried-up lake bed and desert conditions. In 1901 the valley was renamed the Imperial Valley by George Chaffey, one of the chief investors and visionaries who attempted to turn the valley into a garden.[2] And Chaffey meant all that comes to mind with the idea of an imperial valley: "Imperial as in empire, for the million acres of arable land seized from the desert by irrigation were linked in Chaffey's Anglo-Canadian imagination to the march of empire in Canada and Australia in which he played a part. . . . Imperial: not a kingdom inherited, but an empire seized from inhospitable nature through engineering and technology."[3] Technology became the antidote to the unrelenting desert. The dream of technology engulfed what to Chaffey was the nightmare of the desert.

Many have described the Imperial Valley as a desolate and dying area, much like the desert that contains it. Only the hardy survive here. The sun and the clay, the dry climate and the cloudless sky weathered Leonard Knight into the desert father he was. It was in this desert, where few can live at all and even fewer choose to stay, that Knight gained the distance he needed to create his mountain and his utopian vision of the world. Water mattered little to Knight's built environment. Visitors brought him enough bottled water to drink, and he used water from the canal to make his adobe bricks. Knight's understanding of the desert was different from that of most people. To him, the desert offered a space where he could carry on constant conversations with the God he loved and gather the clay he needed to express that love.

Leonard Knight may not have needed much water, but for the last century, the valley itself has been shaped by water and water politics. Water and the lack of water have created the place. Perhaps Marc Reisner said it best when he called the American West a "Cadillac desert," meaning that Americans have built a Cadillac culture in the middle of the desert, a culture that is ultimately unsustainable because there is not enough water. The story of the Imperial Valley, its rise as a contributing agricultural system and its fall from that status, aptly illustrates this unsustainability.

The story of the imperializing of the Imperial Valley begins with European Americans moving westward. Before that time, the indigenous peoples of the region, the ancestors of today's Kumeyaay and Quechan peoples, had adapted to the desert by growing crops near the Colorado River and fishing in Lake Cahuilla, an ancient lake situated in the basin that now houses the Salton Sea.[4] Geologists tell us that at one time the Colorado River made the Salton Sink, the depression that eventually became the Salton Sea, into a huge freshwater lake, filling the area with water when the river changed its course.[5] The river eventually returned to its usual course and the ancient lake dried up, leaving a mineral-rich, dry lake bed on the valley floor.

Unlike the indigenous peoples who adapted their lives and their agricultural practices to the desert environment, European Americans who saw the desert and the dry lake bed immediately wanted to change it. And that impulse remains true to this day. "People say that they 'love the desert,' but few of them love it enough to live there," writes Reisner. "Most people 'love' the desert by driving through it in air-conditioned cars, 'experiencing' its grandeur. That may be some kind of experience, but it is living in a fool's paradise. To *really* experience the desert you have to march right into its white bowl of sky and shape-contorting heat with your mind on your canteen."[6]

Fear of the unrelenting desert and the desire to civilize the untamable, to make a garden of the desert, transformed the American West. George Chaffey and his friend Charles Rockwood had the power to change the Imperial Valley. The two men had a vision of turning the ancient delta into a thriving agricultural region. The only hitch was that the annual rainfall was about 2.4 inches: the western mountains inhibited moisture from the Pacific Ocean from moving that far east. These obstacles did not stop the visionaries; they simply brought water to the region: "By 1901, Rockwood and Chaffey had cut a diversion channel [into the Colorado River], and a good portion of the river was pouring over fields [of the Imperial Valley]. . . . Within eight months, there were two towns, two thousand settlers, and a hundred thousand acres ready for harvesting."[7] Even then, the process of creating an agricultural region was not simple. The channels they created eventually silted up and new channels had to be dug.

Then, in 1905, all hell broke loose. The Colorado River flooded and broke through all of the control mechanisms the engineers had built. The river flooded into the lowest geographical point in the area: the Salton Sink. At its greatest strength, the river flooded 360 million cubic feet per hour into the Imperial Valley.[8] After sixteen months of flooding, and labor and funds from the railroads and the US government, workers were able to stop the flood and encourage the river back to its usual course. During the months of flooding, the river had created a lake about thirty-five miles long and fifteen miles wide. The desert heat could have eventually dried up the mistake lake, but runoff from the irrigation of local farms kept entering the Salton Sea. At the same time that irrigation kept water in the lake, it also increased the salinity of the lake's water. That, along with about six feet of evaporation annually from the desert heat and the fact that the lake has no outlet, meant a rapid rise in the lake's salt content so that today its salinity is close to ocean levels.[9]

The early-twentieth-century attempts to change Southern California into a garden meant that the entire state began to use large portions of the Colorado River's resources. Other states, including Colorado (which contributed half of the water to the river), Wyoming, Utah (which contributed about a third of the water to the river), Arizona, and New Mexico, were not yet populated enough to need the river's water. As California sought to build a dam that would enable it to get through the river's leaner years, it had to negotiate with these other states exactly what its share would be. The original negotiation of the Colorado River Compact took place in 1922. The compact needed ratification by the voters of each of the states. Most of the participating states balked for one reason or another until Congress stepped in, authorizing the Boulder Dam and the All-American Canal (running to Imperial Valley) "on the condition that at least six of the seven states ratif[ied] the compact and that California limit its annual diversion to 4.4 million acre-feet per year."[10] Imperial Valley got its canal, which drew from the Colorado River, ran through portions of Mexico, and then delivered water to the region.[11] With the

All-American Canal, the Imperial Valley became one of the largest irrigation projects in the world. The imperial visionaries had won, it seemed; they had successfully turned the desert into a garden. For a time, anyway.

The Imperial Valley has fields that grow lettuce, carrots, tomatoes, artichokes, asparagus, beans, beets, onions, and broccoli, to name a few crops. It currently grows fruits such as lemons, oranges, grapefruit, nectarines, and tangerines as well as nuts such as pistachios and cashews. The valley also grows "fifty thousand acres of grasses for pasture and seed and plants another eighty thousand in Sudan grass, much of which goes to Japan to fatten Kobe beef." Farmers and ranchers in the Imperial Valley not only grow fruits and vegetables but also house "roughly a million sheep and feedlot cattle, plus dairy cows, swine," and bees.[12] All of this growth in the desert happens because of the water that is brought into the valley from somewhere else. And all of it might be taken away by the demands of urban California on rural California.

San Diego wants to use the water currently being used by farmers in the Imperial Valley. The city does not want to irrigate fields and supplement the Salton Sea but instead supply its ever-growing population with the water it needs. With California already exceeding its allotment of Colorado River water by over 20 percent, and with the other six states now wanting to draw their own allotments from the Colorado River (allotments they were previously willing to sell to the State of California), water from the Imperial Valley seems San Diego's and the state's cheapest option. The city itself imports about 90 percent of the water it uses and so is utterly reliant on imported sources for sustenance.[13] San Diego has presented the transfer of the water as a boon to the Imperial Valley, one that will bring much needed funds into the area.[14] "Under the terms of the deal, Imperial Valley farmers are scheduled to sell San Diego County residents up to 65 billion gallons of water a year for a rough average of $50 million a year, for a 45-year period that could be extended to 75 years," reports one news source.[15] Those in the Imperial Valley who are opposed to the transfer claim that the agreement was signed under duress and that it requires farms to lie fallow, an insult to a territory that has heralded itself as a farming land. Though the dispute has not yet been settled, the controversy exposes the identity contradictions of the Imperial Valley: is it a garden, a land that yields to human cultivation, or a desert that is too wild to be tamed? On this question, the residents of San Diego and the Imperial Valley disagree. Chaffey's dream of the desert blossoming into a rose is slowly starting to turn on itself and the area that used to yield a portion of the nation's agriculture may well turn back into the dust-bowl desert that the imperializers met when they first arrived—the desert where no one wanted to live.

FAILURE AND OPPORTUNITY

The Salton Sea is a travel destination for all sorts of folks who want to see and visit the area that *almost* became the next Palm Springs but did not for a variety of political, economic, and environmental reasons. It is a distinct place in that it was created by an engineering mistake, one that has caused multiple other problems for the area. One of the most obvious problems that visitors to the lake often notice is a distinctly fishy smell coming from the decay of dead tilapia on its banks. The smell and the sights, the sounds and the feel, all result from contradictory desires: to both preserve and use, to both protect and make productive.

After the flooding of the river, an economy cropped up around the Salton Sea, one reliant on both agriculture and tourism. In the mid-twentieth century residents of the Salton Sea area expected it to be the next Palm Springs, and for a time, it seemed that towns like Salton City, located on the lake's western shore, might become just that. Because of the rise in tourism, locals decided it would be nice to stock the lake with fish to create another tourist pull. As early as 1929 the California Department of Fish and Game introduced striped bass to the lake, but none were ever caught. In 1934 the same department stocked the lake with fifteen thousand silver salmon fingerlings. These introductions did not prove particularly fruitful. It was not until the late 1940s and early 1950s that several species—gulf croaker, orange-mouth and gulf-fin corvina, halibut, perch, smelt, tilapia, and several others—were introduced to the lake and thrived.[16] One of the most successful of these species was tilapia. Fishing heightened interest in the spot as a tourist location, causing the local towns to boom in the 1960s and early 1970s.

Dead fish along the banks of the Salton Sea. Photo by author.

Decaying structure at Bombay Beach, Salton Sea. Photo by author.

Mud volcanoes in Imperial County, California. Photo by author.

A flood in 1976 initiated an economic decline from which the area has yet to recover. Tropical storms in both 1976 and 1977 raised water levels so high that the lake covered parts of the towns that sat at its edge. For Salton City, on the western shore, the floods caused property values to plummet. Half of Bombay Beach, a working-class town on the eastern shore of the lake, flooded and has not yet been rebuilt, making the entire place look like a ghost town in an old Western movie or a postapocalyptic remnant of human civilization.

To add insult to injury, the fish that had drawn tourists to the banks of the Salton Sea now repel those same visitors. The sea has too many tilapia, somewhere around one hundred million. That overpopulation, coupled with summer months when the water becomes so warm and so salty that not enough oxygen gets to the fish, means the lake is now known for dead fish, sometimes stacked several feet high on the beach. The water just can't sustain that much life. The fish die, more algae grows, and more food encourages the reproduction of more fish. An ecological problem has arisen in the wake of an attempt to promote tourism.[17]

Some residents in the area want to preserve what wildlife is left after all of the environmental changes. Their hope is that preservation will also promote tourism. The government established a wildlife refuge in 1930, renamed the Sonny Bono Salton Sea National Wildlife Refuge in 1998; the refuge is located on the southern end of the Salton Sea. Just as this region sees the migration of American retirees fleeing the winters in their home states, it also sees the annual migration of birds heading for warmer climes. The refuge is situated in what is called the Pacific Flyway, an important stop in the migration of several species of birds during the winter months, and was initially established as a breeding ground and safe haven for birds and other species, with 32,766 acres set aside. Experts hoped that the geese that were doing such damage to local crops would inhabit the refuge rather than fields. That wish has only partially come true. Because of the increase in the sea's water levels, much of the initial refuge area is covered in water. Currently, only about two thousand acres are managed as wetlands.[18]

In 1996 disaster struck the refuge in the form of avian botulism. This pernicious form of botulism began in the tilapia that had become the diet of the thousands of migrating birds that had incorporated the area into their migratory paths, in part because of the shrinking wetlands in the rest of California. The birds ate the tilapia and died daily by the hundreds. The refuge could not incinerate the bodies fast enough and so they were eaten by maggots, who carried the botulism but were unaffected by it. Those maggots infected other birds, and the death tolls continued to increase. Though park workers were eventually able to control the outbreak, they have not been able to eradicate it entirely and there are minor occurrences each year.[19]

It is not just the refuge that makes the Imperial Valley geographically unique. One of the distinct and most visited features close to Salvation Mountain is a set of mud volcanoes and mud pots. Tourists can head south on CA-111, turn right on a bumpy dirt road, and find, just a few miles away, bubbling cauldrons of mud. The mud pots look like craters full of boiling, dirty water, and the mud volcanoes, or gryphons, are "formed by eruption of highly viscous mud from the top of the structure." The types of mud volcano in the area vary: "Some are actively spewing mud from their vents . . . some have craters at the top that contain small mud lakes that bubble and sometimes spill over the rim of the craters, and some emit only gas or are not active at all." They look like volcanoes in miniature, with hardened, lava-like mud tracing paths down eight- to ten-foot hills. Both phenomena begin below the surface of the earth. The Salton Sea sits between the southern part of the San Andreas Fault and the northern end of the Gulf of California Rift Zone. Part of the basin between the two fault zones, one that includes the gryphons and calderas, is called the Brawley Seismic Zone. Movement and contact of the sediments in the region produce CO_2 gas, which leaks out at the surface. These unusual seeps are some of "the most-visited geologic features in southern California and receive attention almost daily from tourists and geology classes from all over the country."[20]

The natural world defines the human activity in the region even as the peoples of the region continue to shape the natural world. Concern about the ecological safety of the Salton Sea has raised awareness about the area. If current water trends continue, with more water leaving the lake than coming in, great portions of the lake will evaporate and the remaining water will be too salty to sustain much life. The resulting dust storms will likely reach urban areas hundreds of miles away. If water is kept in the region, other problems might arise. Citizens of towns surrounding the Salton Sea seem both hopeful and concerned that the area might return as a tourist attraction. They want the income that tourism would generate but have come to appreciate the freedom and quiet that the mistake lake has brought to their lives.

Success and failure, opportunity and its lack define the region. Those contradictions are reflected in the population that has come to live in the area permanently, despite its summer climate. As of the 2000 US census, over 142,000 people lived in Imperial County. About 24 percent of the population over the age of twenty-five has only an elementary-level education. Another 17 percent has completed some but not all of a high school education. These are high rates compared to California's statistics of 11.5 percent with only an elementary education and about 12 percent with some high school. In Imperial County only 59 percent of the population has a high school diploma.[21] Those educational statistics correlate with statistics relating to low incomes and high unemployment. Imperial County is the fifth-poorest county in the state. Its unemployment rate is averaged at 26.3 percent, the highest of all of California's counties.[22] In 1998 the county's per capita income of $17,353 was only 64 percent of the national level.

These county statistics stem from a few key causes. First and foremost, though the county is primarily oriented toward agriculture, the role of agriculture has been diminishing. Another cause is a combination of several related factors: the "high rate of unemployment, the low level of educational attainment, the very high proportion of the population that does not speak English, the relative youth of the population, and the significantly smaller share of the working age population that works or is looking for work."[23] Much of the labor force in the county is comprised of border crossers who work in several industries in Imperial County. They are primarily in the agricultural industry, though, and Mexicali residents (who live just across the US-Mexican border) make up about 88 percent of the laborers in the county's agriculture.[24] The 2000 census estimated that 65.1 percent of Imperial County inhabitants are of Mexican origin. In the population centers of El Centro, Brawley, and Calexico, that percentage is even higher: 74.6, 73.8, and 95.3 percent respectively.[25] The history of the region, the economic possibilities and restrictions of the space, and its situation on the border between two nations have made it a space of opportunity and failure, of dreams and nightmares.

FREEDOM AND CONSTRAINT

Heading north on Beal Street from Salvation Mountain, one quickly comes across Knight's next-door neighbors, the migrant inhabitants of Slab City, the free RV park built on concrete slabs left behind by the US military. Slab City is known as a community full of retired "snowbirds" (who live across the continent but head to the desert of Southern California during the cold months of the year) and social dropouts who travel around doing odd jobs and eschewing the middle-class lifestyle of economic achievement celebrated by most Americans. Slab City is a unique spot that has been described as a "not so sinister as it is a strange, forlorn quarter of America. It is a town that is not really a town." The town is not really a town because of its shifting cast of characters, its lack of a structured governmental system, and its lack of utilities: "There are no amenities; no potable water, no electricity, no sewage. Groceries can be picked up in town at the grubby market. . . . Gasoline is bought in distant towns like Brawley; prescriptions and liquor are bought in Mexico. Sewage is held in storage tanks or holes in the ground." Although the usual social divisions that make up "civilized" society don't exist, there are still social divisions in Slab City; those who live there year round and those who winter there are two notable groups who view each other with disdain. Slab City also reflects class and status in its geography: "The north side of Main Street is Poverty Flats. The south side, the suburbs, [is] where the relatively well-to-do motorhomies have their dinner dances and clubhouse trailers."[26] And so, even beyond the strictures of the outside world, Slabbies and snowbirds find ways to divide themselves in the middle-of-nowhere desert.

The entrance to Slab City. Photo by author.

Attempting to discard the trappings of civilized society in Slab City often means discarding one's surname for a tagline or handle suited to what you do: Junkyard Joe or Solar Mike, for example. Leonard Knight was not the only artist who called this area of the desert home. A former friend turned rival, Container Charlie, lived in Slab City for a number of years until he died in May 2011. Container Charlie, whose website's first quotation is from Henry David Thoreau—"Disobedience is the true foundation of liberty. The obedient must be slaves"—lived in a place he called "East Jesus," with a population of one and an elevation of seventy-five feet. The directions provided to Charlie's abode are "Middle of nowhere, turn left."[27] One blogger who encountered Charlie in East Jesus explained the name of the place this way: "both a nod to nearby Salvation Mountain, and a playful reference to the expression that indicates somewhere ungodly far away (my Google search's first entry indicated that the expression East Jesus meant 'way the f*ck out there')." In East Jesus, Charlie set up a sculpture garden that visitors could explore, full of art cars, scrap-metal sculptures, and glass artwork. Like Leonard Knight, Container Charlie was committed to the idea of reusing discarded materials in his artwork. His home is its own unique place. One visitor claimed that "you can't let much ruffle you if you want to live in the middle of the desert with no utilities, in a completely open and free community, featuring an assortment of people on the fringes of society. For the most part, residents are pretty cool around there—but still, one needs to protect their home and keep nosy strangers away." This explains the signs I was greeted with upon entering Charlie's place: "PRIVATE PROPERTY: No Trespassing" and "DANGER: Armed and Bitter Libertarian Drunkards Live Here—Trespassers Will Be Used for Target Practice."[28] This type of greeting, though it may be more humorous than most, is not unfamiliar in Slab City. People go there seeking freedom, a world away from civilization, and are willing to defend that way of life.

Three to four thousand people call Slab City home in the winter months. They embrace the place not only because of the weather but also because of its promise of a truly western lifestyle of freedom and individualism. There are few rules at Slab City, where people rely on concepts of integrity, honesty, and honor. This is a place that, according to one resident, has "just the people doing what they want to do." Another inhabitant explained the appeal of the place as "no rules.... No regulatin'.... No one to tell you what to do."[29] A visitor to Slab City described it this way: "They pay no bills and no rent. The residents are left alone to live as they please. The Last Free Place on Earth, they call it, and it is, in every sense of the word."[30]

Juxtaposed with the romance of this western desire to live away from civilization and enter a world of rugged individualized freedoms is a reality of the military industrial complex and governmental mechanisms of control. There are many people in this place who see nothing but reminders that they do not have the freedom of movement or the freedom to choose how they want to live. Not far from Salvation Mountain are two military bases. Navy teams train for land warfare around Niland, California. The Chocolate Mountains form the northwest boundary of the Salton basin. The range houses both US Navy and Marine Corps gunnery areas, which cover several hundred thousand acres of the mountain range. Because the area is used for military practice, it is closed to the public. It is not uncommon to hear planes and helicopters and practice artillery combats echoing off the mountain walls and desert floors as one sits at Salvation Mountain. The training is supposed to hone the skills of patrolling, weaponry, and demolition. Drills allow squads to practice using "pop up targets and pop flares and smoke grenades—all creating confusion and chaos—which emulates the 'fog' of battle pretty well." Squads simulate combat, which enables them to embrace the motto that "the more you sweat in peacetime the less you bleed in war."[31]

The Naval Air Facility (NAF) El Centro is a base that trains soldiers from all of the branches of the armed services. The area's desert climates and topography lend themselves to training soldiers for combat in many of the world's regions. The website for the facility claims that the NAF's mission is to "provide a singularly unique training environment that is appreciated around the world. The proximity to ranges, ability to accurately simulate night field carrier landing practice and the harsh desert environment are capitalized on not only by Navy pilots, but also by pilots from all branches of the services as well as NATO allies. The ranges are a critical piece in the training cycle and one of the few places left where pilots can 'train like they fight.'"[32] The site also claims that it is uniquely suited for what it does: "What makes the NAF so special is its combination of unique climate, vast unobstructed desert terrain, limited non-military air traffic and its own dedicated gunnery and bomb ranges. These factors make NAF El Centro an ideal environment for aerial combat maneuvering, air-to-air gunnery, bombing practice and electronic warfare training."[33] This place is indeed a training ground for war.

Military bases are not the only signs of the military and governmental industrial complex. A few miles south of Salvation Mountain, on CA-111 at the intersection with Sinclair Road, a road leads to the Calipatria State Prison. Opened in 1992, two years before a second state prison, Centinela, opened in the county, the prison sits on more than 1,200 acres. Its staff numbers about 1,100 for its 4,000 male inmates (even though it was initially intended for only 2,300, meaning that as of 2007 it was operating at 181 percent capacity).[34] The prison, which covers 300 acres of the site, houses minimum- to maximum-security inmates. One of its distinct features is a "1.5 million dollar electrified fence system, which actually causes instantaneous death when touched, which is meant to deter inmates from escaping."[35] Because of the overcrowding in maximum-security areas, a small riot broke out in the prison in October 2010, highlighting the problems of California's overpopulated prison system. The prison has been an economic boon to the area, covering a large geographical region and providing many job opportunities for local people. Nonetheless, it serves as a visual marker representing the power of the state to monitor the lives of its citizens and control their movement through space.

Alongside this display of state force lies perhaps the most significant reminder of governmental power and its ability to restrict freedom in the area: Border Patrol stations and agents are everywhere. Much of the patrol's show of force appears to be related to halting immigration from undocumented migrants, but it also works to ensure that the migration of the one million people who legally cross the border between the United States and Mexico each day runs smoothly. This one million is the largest number of people moving between any two countries in the world.[36] In fact, visitors who travel from Salvation Mountain to Bombay Beach on the Salton Sea, about fifteen miles away, must pass a Border Patrol crossing, be questioned, and potentially have their car searched.

This area of the border has witnessed increasing militarization over the past thirty years. In 1986 Congress passed the US Immigration Reform and Control Act, which was an attempt to slow illegal migration across the border by punishing employers of undocumented workers and providing amnesty for undocumented workers who had lived in the United States for four years. This strategy, though it decreased the number of people crossing the border for a few years, ultimately failed to stop the flow of undocumented migrants. Migrants continued to cross the border for dozens of reasons, primarily economic, and did so along the easiest routes—from urban area to urban area. Once a migrant got to an American city, she or he could disappear amid the crowds and find low- or no-skill jobs without drawing the attention that might come in rural areas. In the beginning of the 1990s, on the basis of Border Patrol data, government officials estimated that the majority of unsanctioned crossings along the two-thousand-mile-long border took place in the corridor between Tijuana and San Diego.[37] The Pew Hispanic Center backs up this assessment; it estimates that Mexicans constitute between 50 and 60 percent of the estimated twelve million undocumented foreigners in the United States.[38]

In the mid-1990s two strategies were developed to halt migration through the main corridors from urban area to urban area: Operation Gatekeeper attempted to close passageways between San Diego and Tijuana, and Operation Hold the Line attempted to close the passage of people from Juárez to El Paso in Texas. According to the Department of Justice, the goal of Operation Gatekeeper was "to stem the tide of illegal immigrants crossing the border from Mexico into the United States and to shift the remaining traffic eastward, where the Border Patrol believed it enjoyed a strategic advantage over would-be crossers."[39] There were several justifications, both stated and unstated, that influenced greater attention to heightening border security. Undocumented immigration into California rose during each decade of the late twentieth century. Workers largely took unskilled and semiskilled jobs, jobs Californians did not want, but a recession in the 1990s had massive repercussions for sentiment about immigration. During that same time, Governor Pete Wilson blamed immigration for California's budget crisis. The media

and politicians portrayed immigrants from Mexico as either drug deal-
ers or job stealers and there was a perception that they were draining the
economy, particularly the educational and health-care systems. The feeling many Californians had of being "taken over" was exacerbated by the
shifting ethnic demographics in the region. In 1960 California was one
of the whitest states in the country. By the 1990s it was one of the most
ethnically diverse, with the majority being people of color.[40] Some
Californians began to feel beleaguered and demanded that the government pay more attention to stopping undocumented border crossings.

Monies directed toward the "immigration problem" increased after
the attacks on the World Trade Center on September 11, 2001, and have
only continued to grow since that time, even though the attacks had
nothing to do with policing the border between the United States and
Mexico. In 2003 the federal budget proposed a $2 billion increase for the
Border Patrol. In 2010 President Barack Obama proposed $7.6 billion for
the US Customs and Border Protection agency (which includes the
Border Patrol) and $779.5 million for fencing, infrastructure, and tech-
nology to help police the border. Over the course of the past two decades,
the border went from being a fence with several holes in it to a well-
maintained, twelve-foot-high fence, with cameras and stadium lighting
that ensures people feel *seen*. Much of the fence is topped with coils of
barbed wire, and the technology used by border agents includes under-
ground sensors, infrared scopes, long-range cameras, and lights, so that
even if migrants feel they are not seen, they may well be.[41] All of these
actions on the part of the government provide visual messages to those
who dwell and move through these places: this place needs to be secured,
the fences and patrol officers communicate, and there are insiders and
outsiders, people who are allowed to move through the space and people
who are not.

At the same time, the mode of traveling across the border began to
change: in 1995, 80 percent of people caught attempting to cross the border
illegally were pedestrians, whereas in 2004, 80 percent were in motorized
vehicles of some type.[42] This was accompanied by the post-NAFTA
increase in trade between the United States and Mexico. Around five million cargo trucks cross the border each year. These trucks, along with the

daily migrations of documented border crossers, mean that it is impossible for Border Patrol agents to check each car. There are bottlenecks of vehicles attempting to cross the border each day, so agents must rely on other technologies to aid them in finding undocumented immigrants.[43]

The militarization of the borders surrounding urban areas did not seem to halt migration much; what it did do was push migration toward the unpopulated desert areas east of San Diego and west of Texas. Migrants now have farther to walk or drive—through harsh desert. The militarization of the border with Operations Gatekeeper and Hold the Line "increased the vulnerability and mortality of undocumented immigrants." Estimates suggest that deaths have increased by 500 percent. One historian of the Imperial Valley claims that "there were more than two hundred and fifty illegal-alien deaths along the border from October 2002 until October 2003—a record. Seventy of those corpses were found in the Imperial Valley."[44] And so the romanticized freedom offered in narratives of the American West—the freedom of identity, of activity, and of location—are freedoms realized only by a few inhabitants of the Imperial Valley. Others find only limitations within that space.

Salvation Mountain, then, exists in the borderlands. This area is as much Mexico as it is the United States, even if the Border Patrol is trying to change that reality. The only radio stations around Salvation Mountain carry mariachi music, country music, and evangelical religious programming, representing the various groups of people found here. Spanish and English, and the mix of the two that develops in the borderlands, are spoken everywhere. In a number of the county's towns, "authentic" Mexican restaurants dot all of the main roads and the Latino population is a majority. Salvation Mountain itself seems to reflect the artwork of Mexico. Its use of color and its depiction of the natural world speak the same symbolic language of much popular Mexican art. Clearly, Leonard Knight's artwork was influenced by the borderlands: in its appearance, its use of clay and adobe, and its ability to serve as a symbol that can be interpreted differently by many different viewers.

Salvation Mountain represents the contradictions of its county. It is both the wild, untamable desert and a built environment. It is part sculpture, part painting, part architectural innovation. It is a representation of an Edenic world where everything grows and thrives. It does not use water, though, to build its garden. It uses paint. In its depiction of a mountain with green pine trees and waterfalls cascading down the side and draining into an ocean, the Mountain represents, in its own quirky way, the promise of water in the desert. The dream is of water, blue and white, cascading into an agricultural valley where all things grow. And yet tumbleweeds jut up through cracks in the paint, reminding visitors of the desert's attempts to reclaim the space. In Salvation Mountain, desert and built environment battle one another to claim ownership of the space.

At the same time Salvation Mountain embodies the paradoxes of failure and opportunity and of freedom and constraint. According to all social measures, Leonard Knight was a failure. For decades he had no job, no home to speak of, no property, and no family. In this way, he fit in with some of the occupants of Slab City and of the broader Imperial Valley. Leonard Knight was a migrant searching for the promises that the West has made to Americans for centuries. Yet he saw the desert as an opportunity to escape the world and its measuring sticks of success. He saw in the American West the freedom that he could not find elsewhere. There he found the space to claim a stake in the world, to build his own version of what home and community should be and to keep busy with a singular task to honor his God. It was in the desert that Knight saw an opportunity for daily divine encounters and for true shared community. In this space he redefined success and attempted to create a visionary community with divine love at its foundation. Knight wanted to merge the freedom promised in the West with an understanding of a different world where social status meant nothing because all were loved by God.

Knight's small visionary space is not the only place in the Imperial Valley that embodies the contradictions of the desert. The closest town, Niland, California, also exhibits the contradictions of the area, the dreams of opportunity and the reality of failure. Because the town was central to several railway stops, early-twentieth-century boosters touted Niland as a nexus of the future. In 1930 one booster proclaimed, "Some day Niland's dream of commercial and horticultural greatness will be realized." Another booster argued that "because of its reputed frostless climate the entire district bids fair to become the favored citrus section of the Valley." In 1939 yet another guide stated that Niland had "some of the largest ranches in the valley; on one ranch alone are 4,000 grape-fruit, 18,000 orange, 6,000 lemon and 2,000 tangerine trees."[45] Niland never became a central railroad stop or a citrus dreamland, nor did it ever achieve horticultural greatness. It became a town of a little over one thousand residents that boasts a few restaurants and a market and is the gateway to Salvation Mountain. The majority of Niland's residents live somewhere at or below the national poverty level. Boarded-up build-ings and dilapidated homes line several of the main streets. What the imperialists saw as untapped possibility became a missed opportunity.

Water did not have the effect on the area that the imperialists imag-ined; they could not make the entire desert a garden. They could not even make Niland one. The reality is a run-down, economically depressed area. The reality is a lake so salty that it kills its fish—a lake that may not be around for much longer if the people of San Diego continue to demand the right to drink water from the Colorado River. The reality is a land that cannot offer what the imperialists envisioned. And in the middle of it all is Salvation Mountain, which also offers a different vision of how things ought to be. Salvation Mountain is both Mexico and the United States, both desert and garden, both freedom and constraint, and both failure and opportunity. It embodies the contradictions that define the space around the place.

3

Gift Giving and Mountain Making

Exchange and Sacred Space

When an individual plays a part, he (or she) implicitly requests his
observers to take seriously the impression that is fostered before them.
They are asked to believe that the character they see actually possesses
the attributes he seems to possess, that the task he performs will have
the consequences that are implicitly claimed for it, and that, in general,
matters are what they appear to be.

—DAVID MORGAN, *VISUAL PIETY*

I give . . . and people give . . . [but] you can't out-give God.

—LEONARD KNIGHT

LARRY YUST, A PHOTOGRAPHER hailing from Los Angeles,
spent a lot of time with Leonard Knight over the years. During that time
he recorded the changing landscapes of the mountain and several of
Knight's stories. Knight once told Yust a story about three or four generations of a family who visited Salvation Mountain. The first generation
was represented by a ninety-one-year-old woman, the eldest in the family. Once the family arrived, they began to scurry up the mountain and
explore. The rest of the family left the ninety-one-year-old woman at the
base, claiming "that she was too old" to climb to the top. So Knight went

69

over to her and said, "Well, I'll help you up that mountain if you want to go up there." And the two headed to the top.

When Knight and the woman returned to the bottom of the mountain, "she was the head of the conversation," Knight recalled. "All her family was listening to her. She was the center of that conversation for at least ten minutes, and it really thrilled her heart that she went up there, and it thrilled my heart, too."[1] In this brief account, we begin to see the world that Knight constructed at Salvation Mountain. In his world, those whom society leaves behind or on the margins move to the center and become authoritative voices. Reminiscent of biblical passages that promised that "the last will be first, and the first will be last" and that "the stone the builders rejected has become the cornerstone," Knight constructed a world quite intentionally different from the outside.[2] At Salvation Mountain, Knight created a world in which his life had meaning, and he was able to express his values and his sense of calling in a spatial way.

Religious studies scholar Jonathan Z. Smith tells an unforgettable story in his essay "Map Is Not Territory" that has much to offer us in its understanding of religion and space. Long before Smith was a scholar of religion, he set out to learn about agriculture in order to attend an agricultural school. He interned at a dairy farm with a farmer who, without knowing it, taught Smith a lesson about how the world worked. Each morning Smith marveled at the events that unfolded. At 3:45 a.m. Smith would wake up and start a fire to heat some water so the farmer could wash with warm water and soap before heading out to work. Every morning the farmer went through the ritual of cleansing himself, and every morning he walked outside, picked up a handful of soil and rubbed it all over his hands.

A frustrated Smith finally asked him, "Why do you start each morning by cleaning yourself and then step outside and immediately make yourself dirty?" The farmer reflected on what was to him a preposterous query and replied, "Don't you city boys understand anything? . . . Inside the house it's dirt; outside, it's earth. You must take it off inside to eat and be with your family. You must put it on outside to work and be with the animals."[3]

What to Smith seemed the strangest of activities made absolute sense in the world in which the farmer operated. Later, Smith realized that there is "nothing that is inherently or essentially clean or unclean, sacred or profane. There are only situational or relational categories, mobile boundaries which shift according to the map being employed."[4] That was precisely it; the farmer had created a world in which his life, his work, and his family had meaning. "By limiting the space over which he had dominion, he strove to maximize all of the possibilities of that space," notes Smith, "in both his home and farm, a microcosm in which everything had its place and was fulfilled by keeping its place."[5] The farmer, Smith saw, had created his own map of the world.

As humans produce their maps of the world, they imbue those maps and the spaces in which they dwell with meaning. Humans produce space as they work to own, define, and story it. Religion can often play a crucial role in these practices.[6] Religion happens in space, but space is not merely the setting in which religion happens. Geographer Roger Stump argues that humans seek "spatial realization of their beliefs."[7] They work to make their beliefs feel concrete "by creating worlds in space."[8] Believers construct worlds full of meaning and those worlds then communicate back to them, affirming the belief systems that allowed the worlds to be created.

These theoretical approaches can help us better understand Leonard Knight. While the narratives of freedom found in the American West that draw many people to Salvation Mountain may be romanticized, Knight had to distance himself from his culture in order to set up a world that was meaningful for him. It was in his own space in the middle of nowhere that Knight made a space *his place*. It was not land he owned, but it was land he made his own. In the spring of 2011, when Knight first experienced heart failure, he was reluctant to leave his place. The mountain was the place that made his life significant. At that time his caregiver, Kevin Eubank, convinced him to go to a hospital, where he stayed for three days. Though doctors were reluctant to let him leave, Knight demanded that he be returned to his mountain, his place. In fact, he worried that by going to hospitals and doctors he had somehow communicated to God that he did not trust God's ability to keep him healthy and well. "Now that I've been back here," Knight explained, "my health has been improving every day." According to Knight, the place had made him well; it brought meaning back to his life. The place had made him the *artist* and *prophet* Leonard Knight. And it was in that place, his map of the world, that he intended to die.

Why? Leonard Knight went from being a working-class laborer who did not have a space to call his own in the world to a mapmaker of his own religious reality. At the center of his world lay the mountain, on the site where God had chosen to make his hot-air balloon fail and his truck break down. Leonard Knight understood that he was building a mountain upon the failures that God had chosen for him. In that space, he created a world that was different from the one he had left behind. In that world, he got to say what mattered and what didn't matter. For Knight, what mattered was not social status but one's membership in God's creation. What mattered was not money but gifts. At Salvation Mountain, Leonard Knight created a new world with his pilgrims, one with a different philosophy of how the world should work. He created an alternative space in which spontaneous and ritualized gift giving was the primary activity. In this way, Knight set a boundary around a space and imagined a difference between what was "outside" and what was "inside." Inside represented all that he held precious and dear.[9] In marking the distinction between inside and outside, Knight and his visitors created a powerful prophetic platform from which Knight could critique his culture.

That prophetic platform and the critique Knight made from it is one of the reasons people travel from around the world to visit Salvation Mountain. Knight not only celebrated the little guy on the totem pole, but also created a world that values that little guy. It is only because Knight had a radical vision for his piece of the world that he was able to authentically and consistently critique the capitalist market and the Christian church as an institution—and in order to do so he had to dwell outside of both systems. He had to dwell in the gift.

GIFT GIVING

Knight approached gift giving with a seemingly endless vitality. He believed that his own evangelical work was inspired by the gifts God had given him. His theology centered on the gifts of God and the gratitude inspired by those gifts. For Knight and many religious believers, the relationship between humans and the divine is defined by an understanding of the type of exchange that occurs between the divine and human realms. For many Christians, the death of Jesus is a central component of faith. They interpret the death of Jesus as compensation for a debt humanity owed to God because of sin. In this theology humans are always in debt to a god who gave them something they could never deserve. Instead, Knight understood Jesus's life and death as God's gift to humanity. Though this may seem like a small semantic distinction, the theological ramifications are large. Knight's primary mode of interacting with God was in the posture of gratitude for a supreme gift given. That posture is somewhat different from the posture of a debtor, especially a debtor who can never repay what has been paid. Knight came to his work and his ritual life with an understanding of being the recipient of an eternal gift. His posture of gratitude required him to understand his role in the world as passing the gift along to other humans and responding to God with a sense of gratitude.

To better understand Knight, theorist Lewis Hyde's definition of a gift is helpful: "A gift is a thing we do not get by our own efforts. We cannot buy it; we cannot acquire it through an act of will. It is bestowed upon us."[10] This idea, that one cannot buy but can only receive the gift, lies at the heart of Knight's activities at Salvation Mountain. Knight thrived on the reception of his gift and banked on the idea that visitors would take that gift and carry it out of the middle of nowhere and into their own maps of the world.

Hyde claims that art can often "exist simultaneously in two 'economies,' a market economy and a gift economy. Only one of these is essential, however: a work of art can survive without the market, but where there is no gift there is no art."[11] When people are moved by artwork, they "are grateful that the artist lived, grateful that he labored in the service of his gifts."[12] Because Salvation Mountain was not for sale and because there was no entrance fee, Knight was able to suggest that it lay solely in a gift economy and was not a commodity. In claiming that the mountain could not be bought, Knight was able to take a particular moral stance.

Hyde notes that "religions often prohibit the sale of sacred objects, the implication being that their sanctity is lost if they are bought and sold."[13] By operating through the exchange of gifts rather than within the market economy, Knight was able to set Salvation Mountain apart as a sacred space. It could not be owned, he claimed. It could not be bought. In standing by the gift, Knight had the ability to critique the commodified culture in which he lived.

In fact, Knight did not just stand by the gift, he became part of it by being part of the experience itself. "So many people are removed from their work, their message," claimed one visitor. "Leonard greets you, talks with you. That's part of the art [and] the message."[14] In being a key component of visitors' experience of the artwork, Knight merged his message and his medium. His mountain, as gift, was a moral high ground. In existing outside the regular forms of exchange in American culture, it served as a critique of that culture without anything being said. The mountain can only be appreciated. It is abundance. It is a gift.

Knight called his mountain a "gimme mountain." He would say, "I give . . . and people give me paint . . . [but] you can't out-give God."[15] Here Knight laid out his view of the world as a cycle of gift giving, one that had at its center the theological claim that God is abundance and love. Knight believed that abundance flowed through his paintbrush as he created his mountain, his gift to the world. And yet that gift was not unilateral but reciprocal. One manifestation of this reciprocity is the fact that people brought him the raw materials for the mountain. Visitors felt that they were able to participate in the future of the gift even as they were in the process of receiving all that the gift had to offer.

Knight believed that the sacred place itself takes part in the "gimme" circle that created the mountain. He saw more in this desert spot than do most people, who at first describe it in ways similar to a pilgrim from Baltimore, Maryland, who called it "the blistering, nowhere desert."[16] The place, Knight claimed, gave him the gifts necessary to build a successful mountain. And he trusted that what he needed would be provided one way or another: "If I need something, it just comes in."[17] He spent part of his time scavenging the desert to find discarded "junk" (car windows, truck doors, truck and tractor tires) and dead tree limbs because he believed them to be a key component of his work. Knight often repeated that "the mountain gives me the clay" and that "all the windows you see were out in the desert."[18] He described the circle of gift giving this way: "All the sticks are out in the desert. The mountain gives me the clay. The farmers give me the straw. People give me the paint." Perhaps it is this component of Knight's work, this ritualized gift giving from the surrounding world, that—more than any other—ties his art to *place*.

Knight's mountain was the gift that he offered to people and to God; it was his contribution to what he understood as the circle of gift giving with the mountain at its center. Because of this, Knight spent the money he received from donations to spread the word about his mountain. Pilgrims were offered stacks of postcards, boxes containing picture puzzles, and DVDs titled *A Lifetime of Childlike Faith,* produced by HeuMoore Productions. The film outlines Knight's life story and the story of the mountain itself. These gifts he put out into the world in hopes that they would encourage just one individual to realize God's love.

It was this ritualized gift giving that enabled Knight and his pilgrims to set the mountain apart as a sacred space. With his narratives and his artwork, Knight demarcated the boundaries of his sacred space, but what he did—*what people do*—in that space marked it as sacred as well. In his sacred site Knight set up a gift-exchange system as opposed to a com-modified economic system. This site was necessarily set apart from the economic systems he critiqued. Only in the desert, on land no one wanted or claimed, could Knight construct an alternate map. In a place no one wanted to live, Knight built his gift to humanity. Of course it would be wrong to believe that capitalism does not touch that sacred space. People bought the paint they gave to Knight. Sometimes Knight used the money he received in donations to buy himself a banana at the local grocery store, one of his favorite treats. This is a reminder that sacred and profane are not mutually exclusive categories. As religion is lived in the world, there is a messiness that complicates the neat catego-ries and divisions we like to claim in our speech. That Knight and his pilgrims perceived this place as a place set apart by gift exchange is none-theless critical to our understanding.

Lewis Hyde notes that gift giving challenges the "dominant modes of relating within capitalist societies [in which] calculated or rational self-interest should dominate decisions."[19] In operating as a gift economy, Knight's mountain embodied his own prophetic critique of the capitalist system that divides people and separates the haves from the have-nots. Knight's disdain for the capitalist market was rooted in his theology that God loves everyone equally and requires humans to care for one another. That theology led Knight to believe that money was "filthy lucre" that could corrupt individuals, disrupt communities, and distance humanity from God.

In this way, Knight was not unlike many others who have fled to this desert to escape the evil corruptions of capitalism. Many of these individuals have been pulled by the mythology that it is away from society and civilization and in the wilderness that one can find freedom to live outside of the capitalist world, which, they argue, enslaves people. They critique the rat race, which causes people to focus their lives on amassing as much money as possible in hopes of one day "winning" by having the biggest pile of money. This alternate narrative participated in the mythology of the American West: one can flee capitalism and the rat race to find true freedom. And countless individuals have fled to the West for precisely this reason.

One such individual is the anonymous artist who used the water towers left over from when Slab City was a military base as his canvas. Ask anyone at the Slabs and they'll tell you that the artist fears for his life and doesn't want his name associated with his artwork. After all, the story goes, the government might come after him. From the top of Salvation Mountain, one can see the water towers about a quarter of a mile away. The water tower closest to Salvation Mountain, titled the "Wheel of Kama," pictures beings, often half human and half animal, engaged in all types of sexual activity. The tower's message is a critique of social expectations about sexuality. It offers a positive view of all types of sexuality as it depicts a butterfly and hummingbird, a human and panda, and a giraffe and a goat having pleasurable sexual unions with one another. The water tower farther away from Salvation Mountain is a critique of the ways that government and corporations control American citizens' lives. Pictured as dinosaurs trampling everything in their paths, corporations such as General Motors (GM), Monsanto, Walmart, Disney, Bank of America, and Freddie Mac dominate the tower. The government is shown driving tanks and raining bullets and napalm down on unsuspecting peoples. In fact, the words painted at the top of the artwork command, "Shoot, Claw, Bite, Stone, Rob." These are surely action verbs that communicate the artist's understanding of these corporations and the way they run the world. The artist of these towers found the canvas and the freedom to paint it—no one stopped him, after all—in the same desert where Leonard Knight found the room to build his mountain. The tower's message: corporations and governmental agencies enslave us and rule the world. His fear: someone might hold him accountable for that message.

The "Wheel of Kama" behind Salvation Mountain. Photo by author.

Tower critiquing the power of corporations. Photo by author.

Another artist, briefly mentioned in chapter 2, also fled to the same few square miles of desert to create his artwork. That artist, known locally as Container Charlie (Charles Russell, 1965–2011), initially set up shop at Salvation Mountain, where he helped Leonard with the mountain and worked on his own artwork. After staying at the mountain for some time, Charlie and Leonard had an artistic and roommate-related falling out. Perhaps there was only room for one artist at Salvation Mountain. Knight became convinced that Charlie was evil and Charlie moved farther into Slab City and named his abode East Jesus to poke fun at his old roommate. Even though they had a falling out, there are general themes that run throughout the two artists' works. They moved to the desert to create art with these themes and they clearly were inspired by the desert, its peoples, and all of the waste and trash produced—they sought to make art out of what society had discarded.

Container Charlie's television sculpture. Photo by author.

Container Charlie's artwork critiques American culture from head to toe: he loathed the media and felt that television corrupts American minds, he disliked the way the US government wages wars that cost the lives of young Americans, and he critiqued the wastefulness of American society by using its "junk" to make his art. One piece of art is a wall of broken television sets with messages painted onto their screens: "Badvertising" and "Entertainment Is Crap" are intermingled with prophetic messages such as "Television Will Not Be Revolutionized" and "Inaccurate Representation of Reality" as well as an order to "Get off the couch." Statue soldiers are depicted with televisions for brains, motherboards for hearts, and weapons aimed at the viewer, suggesting that the government and media dehumanize soldiers and make them killing machines. A sculpture of a worker illustrates that Americans work themselves to death for nothing except a loss of dreams and body parts. While Charlie hated the way corporations,

A sculpture created by Container Charlie. Photo by author.

media, and the government have, from his perspective, ruined Americans, he still celebrated the American ideals of freedom and individuality. "Down the Rabbit Hole we all must go," claims Charlie's work. It asks viewers if they have "questioned reality." It assures them that they should follow wherever life leads them because "there are no wrong roads to any-where." They simply need to "answer the call."

Charlie's art critiques how the masses blindly follow what they are told, while celebrating the individuality and spirit he found in the desert, away from society. It is this philosophy that Leonard Knight also embraced. He did so from a different perspective, certainly, but with many of the same intentions. Knight based his criticism in his under-standing of what Jesus taught. Charlie's foundation is the American philosophical tradition of Thoreau and the like who dreamed of freedom in the wilderness. Knight too would claim this philosophy, even if he hadn't ever read these authors, but he would trace the ideas back to Jesus. Knight believed that the pursuit of that freedom and its twin, the neces-sary critique of capitalism, stemmed from the works of Jesus of Nazareth, who overturned the money changers' tables when they sought to profane what was holy.

And so he pursued that lifestyle and generated the rituals that invited visitors into the alternative world of gift giving. Though Knight accepted monetary gifts, he did not expect them. The most important things he asked pilgrims to bring were "a camera and a smile." His Social Security checks allowed him to survive—all he really needed was food—because his home was his mountain and he had no need for material things. That fact let him set himself apart and critique the larger culture in which he lived.

Pilgrims frequently appreciated this message from Knight, and some came just to hear him speak on this issue. One pilgrim noted that "living in the simplest conditions imaginable (well, within a developed nation, anyway), Leonard devotes his life to glorifying God by adding to Salvation Mountain. It makes him happy." This same pilgrim saw Knight as one who stood apart from his culture and found it "refreshing, in this stuff-driven, accumulative world of ours, to spend time with someone who delights in his life because of his service, instead of possessions."[20]

After visiting the mountain, another pilgrim explained that those in her group "couldn't contain our smiles when we were with Leonard. He overflows with joy, and it's catching." Her experience led her to quote a passage from Psalms: "You have given me greater joy than those who have abundant harvests of grain and new wine. In peace I will lie down and sleep, for You alone, O Lord, will keep me safe."[21] This passage seems an appropriate description of Knight's view of the world. Believing in a God of abundance who would provide for him, Knight ventured into the desert without a plan. He trusted and never went hungry for long, confirming to his mind the claim that God would provide and did indeed have a plan. Knight's God critiques those who hoard wealth, who care about fancy cars and big homes. Knight's God gives gifts.

Most important for appreciating what occurs at Salvation Mountain, a gift must be understood as creating a relationship between the giver and the recipient. That relationship is necessarily defined by the gift. Relying on the work of theorist Marcel Mauss, anthropologist Karen Sykes has noted that gifts challenge the predominant modes of exchange in capitalist cultures. The gift "contradicts the assumption that human relationships aim towards only utilitarian ends." A gift, then, is able to make "the ideal relationship a material fact" in a way that the exchange of goods in a market economy does not.[22] The nature of a particular gift also sets up the *type* of relationship that the giver hopes to create. Giving is more than the transaction of an object; "how people give and receive is a matter of what kind of relationships they imagine they make and keep with each other; immediately immaterial or ideal concerns become a part of the issue."[23]

Knight's gift of himself in his mountain was offered to other humans as a material fact representing what he believed was the immaterial reality of God's love. Knight believed God gifted him with the ability to create the mountain for precisely this reason: to serve as material evidence of an immaterial reality. His mountain is an offering, an invitation to a relationship. The type of relationship is demonstrated by the message written on the gift. He hoped that people would leave the mountain understanding that God desires love rather than money to be the primary motivating force in the world. Knight's gift was persuasive precisely because the message, the medium, and the man were all communicating the same ideals.

In this way Knight cemented his status as a prophetic speaker. He situated his mountain over and against the larger culture and its modes of exchange. By enacting gift exchange with visitors, Knight and his pilgrims *created a world* that imagined human interaction in different ways. Because Knight lived at the mountain, he had a particularly powerful platform. He chose to live the gift and to work toward enacting a different world. People came from around the world to hear his critique of the world that they live in. They took his prophetic message back to their worlds and perhaps enacted some of that vision there.

In exchanging gifts Knight not only offered a critique of capitalist economies that set up and maintain social hierarchies but also critiqued institutional churches. *This* is the way that true Christians act, claimed Knight and his visitors. They give gifts and they give relationships. Knight did not attend church. He was afraid that some church would attempt to "own" him and make the mountain's message about the church rather than about God. He did not study what various intellectuals had said about particular biblical passages. He did not participate in a hierarchical Christian community. In refusing to do these activities, he suggested that being Christlike was celebrating the gift and passing it along.

Knight's mountain also offered an alternative theology to the one found in many churches: Knight's message was that God's love extends to all human beings. For many of the pilgrims I spoke with, the experience of being at Salvation Mountain was one of being accepted as an equal. At the mountain, only first names are used and the social status one holds in the outside world does not matter. The socially reinforced hierarchies of identity based on class, race, educational level, and gender were of no concern to Knight. In particular, Knight dismissed claims that education grants religious authority: "All the big churches and all their la-de-da expenses and their brains they got education and they got master's degrees. Hogwash. Where does it say that you've got to go to college and be smart to love Jesus?"[24]

Knight's emphasis on God's egalitarian love comes through most clearly in his message about young people, people society thinks will never do much with their lives. Instead, Knight said young people will carry forth the millennial message of love and peace. In fact, Knight declared the younger generation to be pivotal actors in bringing forth the new millennium. One visitor posted on Facebook about his experience of Knight's message about young people. He recalled that when he arrived, Leonard was talking to some other visitors but that "when a few of us younger folks walked up . . . Leonard stop[ped] talking with the other people and came over to us saying, 'I love when young people come to the mountain.'" This visitor recalled that this welcome was "a very touching and life changing experience."[25]

When pilgrims accept Knight's critique of social hierarchies and when they embrace his message about the importance of universal love, they enter into the cycle of gift giving. Feeling as though Knight had given something to them—either religiously, artistically, or both—they often desired to give something back. Paint and money were the two most popular material items to leave at Salvation Mountain. Pilgrims brought paint to donate to the cause so "this awesome place can continue on."[26] For similar reasons they left money—to care for both the mountain and the artist. And finally, numerous pilgrims believed they left behind intangible items such as "footsteps up the yellow-brick road" or "my presence" or "a part of my heart."[27]

Knight's pilgrims did more than just bring physical gifts. They also continued the notion of gift, extending it beyond the perimeter of Salvation Mountain by carrying Knight's story and images of the mountain back home with them. One pilgrim described Knight's work as "the highest call I have ever seen." That pilgrim, along with many others, held the sentiment that "I'm not really leaving . . . much, but rather taking *a lot with me*. Every detail about this place, including Leonard, will be spread with my friends and family."[28] A musician who came to visit the mountain explained that "the whole thing is meaningful; we were greeted with open, welcome arms."[29] That same artist saw a kindred spirit in Leonard Knight, one who used art to communicate a message of love binding all of humanity together. That artist left inspired by the abundance of spirit and love he felt at Salvation Mountain, ready to transmit that love through his work.

These are not the only immaterial gifts pilgrims offered. In an unstated way, they offered to Knight the gifts of witness and presence. They bore witness to Knight's narrative of his own conversion, and their presence

served as an affirmation of the validity of Knight's message and his artwork. They gifted Knight with relationship. The primary activities of that
relationship were *listening to* and *sharing* stories. Through that relationship they affirmed Knight's narratives and subsequently his identity. They
confirmed that the mountain defined Knight's identity and that he derived
his authority from experience rather than formal education. They confirmed that he was an artist whose creativity rather than any formal training defined his status.[30] Because the pilgrims came to see the mountain,
Knight knew that the site was sacred, not profane, that he spoke with a
prophetic voice and was not a fraud, and that the mountain was art, not
toxic junk.

Knight's relationship with the pilgrims—as both givers and receiv-
ers—was solidified in the exchange. His gift, the mountain, had the
potential to increase as more people became aware of it. This increase
occurred through Knight's dissemination of his story and through the
image of the mountain itself. The stories of Knight and the mountain that
the pilgrims took with them and told to others became gifts in their own
right. In this way, the cycle of gift giving radiated beyond the sacred space
that Knight demarcated and accompanied pilgrims as they returned to
their world. As the gift exchange moved beyond the exchange between
two individuals, it functioned in precisely the way Knight hoped it would:
he envisioned a millennial future when God's love descends and spreads
throughout the world. As pilgrims left with images and stories about a
man so committed to this message that he spent thirty years in the desert
building a mountain for God, they spread his message about a new vision
of the future. Knight's faith played a role in this too. As Lewis Hyde
argues, "Bad faith suspects that the gift will not come back, that things
won't work out, that there is a scarcity so great in the world that it will
devour whatever gifts appear. In bad faith the circle is broken."[31]

It was faith that Knight had in spades. His gift to humanity, his
mountain, served as evidence to him that divine love would win out.
Knight banked on the hope that his mountain "can reproduce the gifted
state in the audience that receives it."[32] And that the audience would
then reenter the world that he critiqued and offer the gift of love as a
counter to the social structures they lived in.

DWELLING IN THE GIFT, DWELLING IN THE SACRED

The cycle of gift giving and its creation of sacred space extended beyond Knight and his mountain to his circle of friends, especially to friends who chose to live at Salvation Mountain for a time. These people chose to dwell in the gift, and they provided Knight with relationships that extended beyond an afternoon of shared experiences. An example of this gift community is the community of three who lived together at Salvation Mountain during 2010 and 2011. Aside from Knight, there was Kevin Eubank, who died in December 2011. Eubank was a retired social worker who chose to live not far from the mountain in his own RV and come daily to take Knight swimming, to run errands, and to generally look after Knight's well-being. Eubank took on this unpaid role out of concern that Knight's health had been declining and that he had been taken advantage of by individuals who were attempting to profit from the mountain. Whereas Eubank went to Salvation Mountain with the intention of staying and helping Knight, the third person, Mike Phippen, did not plan to stay when he bicycled out to Salvation Mountain for an afternoon visit. Phippen had heard about an artist who was Christian, like he was, sending God's message to the world through a mountain, and so he decided to check him out. The fact that Phippen stayed for months shows just how profound his experiences in the space were. Knight's theology, his vision and his warmth, convinced Phippen to stay at the mountain, where he was drawn to the rituals of gift giving and storytelling. I offer the stories of these men in detail because they illuminate further the nature of Salvation Mountain, of Knight himself, and the way gift giving creates sacred space. By dwelling in the gift, the three men together created an alternative community that lived outside of the social expectations of their culture and relied on gifts as its form of exchange.

Kevin Eubank did not plan to live in the middle-of-nowhere desert taking care of a prophet-like desert father in the final years of his life. But it fit well with the kinds of work he had done throughout his career, the majority of which was spent providing services for the homeless. Eubank first worked in New York City, where what he did, though often fulfilling, felt like a drop in the bucket in a city whose homeless community had only grown over the decades. He remembered seeing many homeless folks arrive at the shelters he helped run and watching them turn their lives and circumstances around, using a stable address to help find training and work, slowly moving out of the shelter. He remembered even more people cycling through the shelter, the victims of addiction, poverty, and bad luck. He wanted to help them all, but knew the roots of the problem were systemic in the culture. He was satisfied with helping as many as possible while criticizing what was wrong with a society that allowed so many of its citizens to live this way. As the work began to take its toll on Eubank's physical and emotional well-being, he decided to move west to New Mexico, where he first spent a year at a mountain retreat and then took a job as an executive director of a Navajo multiservice agency. Once again, he hoped to help and serve people who were not born into a privileged world.

In 2009 Eubank came to another turning point in his life. He felt alone. His son had moved to Texas and started his adult life in earnest and Eubank himself was experiencing heart failure, confirming that the work he was doing was too much for him physically. Not knowing what to do next, Eubank headed out to the desert in his RV, thinking that some time at Slab City and a visit with Leonard Knight might help.

Slab City and Salvation Mountain were not new to Eubank. In fact, he had visited both almost every year from 1993 on in an effort to "explore some of the communities that were directly affected by the political and ecological situations there." In 1993 Eubank saw Salvation Mountain and met Knight, who "gave . . . a welcome and a tour and spoke about God and loving people." Eubank admitted that he "was hooked" early on because Knight "made [him] feel completely special and appreciated just for dropping by." After having witnessed hundreds of interactions between Knight and pilgrims, Eubank recalled that his "earliest experience was the same as that of hundreds of thousands before and since."[33]

His familiarity with the region meant that Eubank knew the power of the desert, with its unique set of freedoms and constraints. He saw the desert as "a place of constant change . . . never really the same from day to day." Knowing that his life was at a turning point, he found the desert precisely the kind of place he needed to be. Taught by the desert's "shift-ing sands" and winds that "arrive from all directions," Eubank saw that emotions too "rise to the surface and sink into oblivion as quickly as they come."[34] It seemed that the desert's uncompromising change and its relentless heat forced people to reckon with the truthfulness of their lives. It is a region that calls people to account, and that is precisely why Eubank chose the desert when he was going through a difficult period of change in his life.

During his visit, Eubank realized that Knight needed help from some-one. He was aging, experiencing dimming eyesight and poor hearing. Knight's difficulties were exacerbated by the fact that he was not willing to leave the mountain or visit doctors, feeling like the best medicine was a strong faith in God. His medical problems were further compounded by the fact that Knight had, according to Eubank, about one thousand weekly visitors to the mountain. "He was really wearing himself out giving every-one a tour," Eubank recalled. Knight "was fairly manic about it and would nearly pass out by 5 p.m." Because of his declining health, Knight also became an easy target for petty thieves who needed cash. Everyone around Salvation Mountain knew that pilgrims often left Knight with small-dollar gifts demonstrating their appreciation, money that he often shoved in his front pocket, or his shoe, to be found and pooled later. A forgetful Knight would often be surprised to take his shoe off at the end of the day and find a handful of one-dollar bills that he had placed there earlier that same day. Knight had no way to defend himself from thieves and often handed over the money, experiencing some physical abuse in the exchanges.

Eubank saw someone whom he had always admired in need of assis-tance: "I couldn't leave him alone in that environment. How could I?" When Eubank saw a need for assistance, he filled it and vowed to "stay with Leonard until his death" because "he deserves to be cared for and comfortable after the enormous gift he has given us all, and especially me."[35] For Eubank, then, care for Knight was part of the reciprocity of gift giving. To participate in the gift, Eubank dwelt in what he had come to believe was sacred space.

By all accounts, Eubank was not a religious man. He said he found too many hypocrites among the people who most strenuously proclaimed their religious beliefs. He was turned off by the message that he found in the Christian community—a message of exclusion. And to add insult to injury, Eubank believed Christians were using Jesus to promote that exclusivism. Yet he was drawn to the inclusive message of Knight's faith. "Without question," Eubank claimed, "the thing that speaks to me most is Leonard's belief that *all people* are loved by God and that all people are loved regardless of religion, personal preference or edict from any man or church. All people."[36]

This message is precisely what Eubank saw as Knight's gift to the world—an inclusive love for all people. And this is what Eubank focused on in Knight's theology, that no matter what race, gender, creed, *or religion* one is, one is loved by God. For Eubank, Knight's mountain represented "the achievements of the single most successful common man." Eubank believed that the mountain "is so much more than just a work of art . . . [it] is the living room of a man who has chosen to live his life wide open for all to see." Where Eubank saw the churches falling into hypocritical misuse of the Bible, even though it was not a particularly sacred text to him, he *knew* that Knight had chosen "to live the words of Jesus without interpretation, as they are. Love one another. . . . Embrace gratitude."[37] For Eubank, this was a message that did not have to be rooted in Christianity but was one that got at the essence of all religious traditions, got at the core of what makes a good life, a life well worth living. Eubank claimed that the mountain reminded him of "what is important in life and what is not."

Eubank enjoyed a special relationship with Knight. He, more than almost anyone, knew how difficult Knight could be. In fact, at one point Knight grew angry with Eubank for trying to tell him what to do. The two men lived next to one another without speaking for several weeks while Knight "got over" his anger and saw that no matter what he did to push Eubank away, he would continue to stay. While Knight was a welcoming soul to all pilgrims who come to the mountain, that type of public life for a private individual was exhausting. On top of that, Knight spent the past thirty years of his life living "his way" and not having to account for his choices or his behavior to anyone else. This made him the warm, loving person he was, but it could also make him someone with whom it was hard to have an extended relationship. Eubank described Knight as "someone who moved me and pissed me off, used me and loved me and told me so . . . the grandfather I never knew [and] the sage I have always looked for."[38] Knight's life was an example "of a life well lived," one that embodied all that was good and right in the world. The promise of a heavenly reward or a future age of happiness did not speak to Eubank; rather, it was Knight's message about a life worth living and what that life may look like that mattered.

Eubank moved to the desert to care for a desert grandfather and to live in friendship with a man who lived love. That was his gift, which he gave out of gratitude for all that Leonard had given to him and to the world.

A theology of action compelled Mike Phippen to stay at Salvation Mountain for several months and provided him a sense of mission at a moment in his life when he was feeling called in new directions. Phippen grew up in Colorado and stayed there for a few years of college. Eventually, though, he moved to Chicago, where he joined the Jesus People, a group that sprang from the Jesus movement, which began in late 1960s America. Seeking the true spirituality in Christianity, the Jesus People wanted to bring the United States another revival and in so doing brought it "another conception of Jesus tailor-made for its time." Group members attempted to separate Jesus from the institutional church, which seemed bogged down by creeds, rules, and behavioral expectations. Their only behavioral expectation was that one *live* like Jesus did. And in their common imagination and shared social vision, Jesus was the best of the hippies, eschewing the norms of middle-class America, working with the poor, and generally being good.

On a spiritual level, the group traced its origins back to Jesus and the apostles; as a movement it could trace its roots to San Francisco's Haight-Ashbury district in 1967. There, Elizabeth and Ted Wise, two former drug users turned born-again Christians, founded a coffeehouse called the Living Room. The Wises started their ministry to drug addicts, asking people to get high on Jesus rather than on any of a number of drugs. The Wises' Jesus "rejected marijuana, acid, and heroin, but he embraced enthusiastically the slang, clothes, and music of hippiedom."[39] Their followers committed to imitating Jesus; for them, this entailed an expectation that "they dress like Jesus . . . [and tramp] around the Haight preaching Jesus . . . as their Savior." The Californian climate pervaded their ethos. They described Jesus "not as a distant divinity but as a near and dear friend they could know and love and imitate."[40] For some, Jesus was a political activist, challenging the politics of "the man"; for others, he was living with the poor, feeding the poor, and loving his life. For many Jesus People, a key biblical passage was Matthew 8:20: "Foxes have holes, and birds of the air have nests, but the Son of man has nowhere to lay his head."[41] Theirs was a Jesus on the move, committing himself to no institutions but dedicating himself to helping others.

That lifestyle came at a price, the price being that the group eventually had to become an institution of sorts: Jesus People USA (JPUSA). Founded in the 1970s as a band of like-minded members, one that eventually moved eastward, JPUSA and its groupies "sold their bus and settled into a Chicago-based community."[42] Even though the group institutionalized to a degree, it did not lose its diversity—JPUSA communities across the country took on their own distinctive flavors. One point of disagreement was whether or not they accepted a theology of speaking in tongues. Some believed that it was a manifestation of the Holy Spirit, others that it might interrupt the true work of the spirit. On issues such as these they could not agree. What is clear is that their understandings of who Jesus was came to dominate how they lived their lives.

Phippen joined the Chicago JPUSA because he felt tied to their commitment to live their religious beliefs—to live as best they could, as they believed that Jesus had. And it was with this group that he spent nearly sixteen years of his life. During that time Phippen worked odd jobs, most often as a roofer, plumber, and delivery guy. Phippen also had a knack for fixing old cars. People would give him their old junky ones, letting him restore and sell them. The Chicago community allowed its members to keep their own bank accounts while also expecting that they would contribute most of their income to the group as a whole. Because of the latter practice, the group was able to pool its money and purchase an old hotel. Members converted the top three floors into low-income housing for retired people that the JPUSA members serviced, and kept the bottom floors to house Jesus People members. Families and single women lived in the old hotel, and members who were single men had quarters in the next building over.

Phippen had not planned on leaving the Jesus People, but a few things brought about his journey westward, eventually landing him at Salvation Mountain. He began to feel that JPUSA had started to change its values, becoming more family oriented and "settled" in a particular lifestyle. At the same time, he started to feel that he might need a change, a return to a more nomadic life of going out and helping those who needed help. During the midst of this questioning, a friend from New Orleans asked him if he "was getting 'institutionalized' at Jesus People." Phippen did not feel like he could give his friend "an honest No," nor could he imagine a future at JPUSA. "It was like fighting an upstream current, [a] constant struggle in which I saw no future for me."[43]

And so Phippen set out, deciding to cycle to the American West and let his bicycle and God lead him wherever they would. Phippen took his time, making his way first to Colorado and then to California; what stood out to him most along the way was that "everyone has a story." He met "so many amazing people across this land. Each of them [with] a life to live and a story to tell."[44] The stories are precisely what compelled Phippen to love the rather itinerant life he has led and to cherish his time at Salvation Mountain. There, he heard stories in spades—Leonard Knight's, Kevin Eubank's, and those of all of the visitors who ambled up to the mountain on any given day. And it is stories that Phippen recognizes give people meaning. This is precisely why he would spend time during his day reading biblical passages to Knight, whose eyes no longer allowed him to read them for himself. Phippen read to Knight because he knew how important the stories were to making Knight who he was.

Phippen has his own story of religious experience at Salvation Mountain, and it is that story that motivated him to see the space as sacred and to stay for a time. On a whim Phippen decided to visit the mountain, seeing it only as part of one day's journey, not expecting it to be a dwelling space. Phippen's first experience of the mountain was one of "joy and wonder." He was "glad that someone decided to spend so much time on creating a beautiful place," a place with a message that was in line with Phippen's theology: God is love. He found Salvation Mountain to be a special manifestation of divine love in the world. Phippen's favorite parts of the mountain included the "straight up John 3:16 and the Lord's Prayer" along with the "virtue tree" in the alcove, which recalls faith, love, joy, goodness, meekness, peace, temperance, long-suffering, and gentleness as Christian virtues. He enjoyed those aspects of the mountain most because they came from an artist with a "heart of love and simplicity." One whose message is "disarming in its presentation."[45]

Phippen's experience of the mountain was not all that different from the experiences of other pilgrims who visit the site. But two aspects of it remain distinct. First, Phippen did not know what God intended for the next phase of his life, did not know what *place* God was calling him to live. Second, Phippen had a profound religious experience of his own in precisely the same space that Knight had.

While Phippen wandered around the mountain and appreciated its joy and wonder, he saw Knight repainting the red heart right on the center of the front of the mountain, the heart that contains the words of the sinner's prayer. As he went up to thank Knight for the mountain and for all of his hard work, Knight asked Phippen if he would like to help paint the heart. "Don't you think you should get a brush and help me paint this?" Knight asked. Phippen declined, knowing that he had only planned to spend part of the day there. As Phippen walked away, he had a "conviction" in his heart that told him he was meant to stay. For Phippen, well versed in the language of evangelical experience and convicted hearts, God *called* him to stay, to offer his time and his life to Knight and the mountain: to allow himself to be profoundly transformed by it. And so Phippen listened to his heart, turned around, and picked up a paintbrush, forming a close relationship with Knight in the process.

Phippen also saw in Knight a friendly spirit who believed in the gift of tongues provided by the Holy Spirit. The two men bonded over their shared beliefs: of being born again in the spirit, of having their beliefs manifested in the gifts of tongues, and of believing that Christ was the way to salvation. Theirs was a friendship of shared theology. Knight might well have lived Phippen's life if he had been born twenty years later, in time to join groups like the Jesus People. Instead he went into the desert, where Phippen joined him for a time, to live alone and in a chosen community of three who cared for one another and shared the gift of that care, no matter what its inspiration.

Transformation is precisely what moved Phippen when he took up residence at Salvation Mountain. During his time there he lived in one of the old vans behind the mountain. Phippen loved to be present when "someone [was] deeply moved by Leonard and the Mountain." He remembered a time when pilgrims arrived on Good Friday and prayed with Leonard. Phippen "felt like God's spirit was . . . in us."[46] Their shared theology allowed Phippen to see and feel shared experiences in the same language that Knight did—and to be transformed by those shared experiences.

What made Phippen stay, especially when his visit first appeared to be only an afternoon's pit stop in a new and ongoing journey? Phippen stayed because his theology, his understanding of who God is and how God calls people, compelled him to do so. Knight and Eubank asked Phippen to stay, needing a third set of hands to care for the mountain and for Knight in his declining health. Phippen believed that "God's love is expressed in action." And so his commitment to Knight and to Eubank *was* his religion. Phippen stayed because he knew that "it's hard to say God is love and walk away from someone who needs help." And when he said it, he did not mean just Knight, but Eubank as well.[47]

Phippen's theological perspectives are clearly shaped by evangelical Christianity, with its notions of calling and religious experience, and by the Jesus People, who, shaped by the 1960s, believe that theology is nothing if it is not lived in the world. Where Knight escaped to the desert to *live* his understanding of God, Phippen moved to the city in order to *live* his understanding of God. When Phippen met Knight, it was a match made in heaven. Both valued stories and experiences as the heart of true religion. Both believed that the core of Christianity is a nonjudgmental message of God's love. They lived together because both came to believe that the space and the message were mutually reinforcing one another.

Eubank and Phippen stand out from others because of their choices to stay at the mountain, to dwell there if only for a time. Both were pilgrims to the place in their own way, but while pilgrims choose to visit the sacred—to visit prophets they believe know divine truth better than other humans, or to visit a space where they believe the divine has manifested itself in the world in a special way—Eubank and Phippen stayed. They chose to dwell in the gift and in the sacred. What sets that decision apart?

In part, the two men were able to make that decision because they did not have—chose not to have—the expectations placed on them that most men of their age do. They had families, but not families that met the traditional notions of the nuclear family. They worked, but they did not necessarily receive compensation for that work. Both of them embraced work for work's sake. They enjoyed feeling that their work was useful. Both Eubank and Phippen tapped into not only the philosophy of Salvation Mountain but also the philosophy or spirit celebrated in Imperial Valley— of freedom, of changed expectations, of living outside the boundaries of cultural norms. The two also tended to see life as a journey—toward God or toward more meaning and satisfaction, toward the "real." Their journeys led them to Salvation Mountain, just as Knight's did. He made the place; they helped him maintain it. They did so with paintbrushes and cooked dinners, but even more, they did so with shared stories about how the place pulled them to it. They did so by telling other people why they stayed.

Both Eubank and Phippen chose to stay at Salvation Mountain because they viewed it as sacred space. For Eubank, the mountain was a place that represented all that is good in humanity, all that has been sullied by institutions and economic and political interests. For him, Knight represented all that is good in the human spirit: a warm, welcoming, gracious man who opened himself to others so that they might share in his vision in the world. Eubank stayed because of the inclusive vision Knight offered, the world of the gift.

Phippen stayed because his vision was rooted in the biblical stories about Jesus. He valued Knight as a man who lived life the way Jesus did. Phippen himself was trying, as best he could, to live life as he believed

Jesus did, which required knowing and loving one's neighbors, something Phippen saw in that space. At Salvation Mountain, he saw a genuine Christlike vision. In Knight he found a kindred spirit, one who knew about the gifts of tongues and the power of Jesus's death to offer salvation for humanity.

Eubank and Phippen also stayed because Knight needed them to stay in order to maintain his vision and live at his mountain. They chose to dwell in his gift economy and extend the gift back to Knight in profound ways. They knew the value of community, and they gifted Knight with a sustained community when he was most accustomed to brief relationships with visitors. They participated in the gift and were inheritors of Knight's vision. The truth of what Leonard Knight created is further corroborated by these sojourners, by the time and effort they put forth.

In many ways, Knight was a modern-day desert father, one who attempted to flee the trappings of a materialistic world. This man imagined an omnipotent, all-powerful, all-knowing Creator who "made the Atlantic Ocean and the Pacific Ocean. He put the Grand Canyon in between it."[48] With that understanding of the divine, Knight had no problem imagining a God who brought him to the middle-of-nowhere desert to build a mountain (after a try or two) that could proclaim to the world the universal love of the divine. He also did not doubt that just when he needed them, it was God who sent two men to help him care for the mountain and tend to the gift. It is for this reason, as well as the unique traits of the mountain, that pilgrims from around the world drive two and a half hours east from San Diego in order to see an artificial mountain. They come to enter into Knight's alternate map of the world.

4

When Prophet Meets Exile

Salvation Mountain and the
Paradox of Freedom in the American West

The west *is* the best.

—ALEXANDER SUPERTRAMP

To the desert go prophets and hermits;
through deserts go pilgrims and exiles.

—PAUL SHEPARD, *MAN IN THE LANDSCAPE*

IN JANUARY 1993, *OUTSIDE* magazine published an article titled "Death of an Innocent." Written by Jon Krakauer, the article detailed the final two years of Christopher J. McCandless's life, during which he traveled across the American West in search of himself. That journey, inspired by the philosophical perspectives of his favorite authors—Leo Tolstoy, Jack London, and Henry David Thoreau—eventually landed McCandless in the Alaskan wilderness, away from all the trappings of civilization and in search of his "great Alaskan adventure." Like so many before him, McCandless believed he had to escape from civilization in order to truly find himself, and so he trekked into the American West. He died in the Alaskan wilderness, not far from the medical and food supplies that might have saved his life. McCandless did not become one of the nameless individuals who failed in the West. Rather, because Krakauer told his story and because that story resonated with the American imagination of the wilderness and its function in forming identity, McCandless became a romantic, modern-day American hero.

As the stuff of modern American legend, McCandless fared pretty well. Krakauer's article in *Outside* "generated more mail than any other article in the magazine's history."[1] That popularity and Krakauer's own sense that he was not finished telling the story led him to write a book about McCandless's life. *Into the Wild* told McCandless's story in more detail and compared him to other American adventurers. Published in 1996, the book immediately became a best seller and stayed on the list for more than two years.[2]

One of the readers of Krakauer's story was Academy Award–winning actor and director Sean Penn, who turned the book into a major motion picture. Krakauer's book made a strong impression on Penn, who decided immediately to make a film based on McCandless's life.[3] According to Penn, he "read the book when it came out . . . read it twice in a row [and] started to get the rights to it the next day." Like so many other Americans, Penn was drawn to McCandless's story because it was "about somebody who had a will that is so uncommon today, a lack of addiction to comfort, that is so uncommon and is so necessary to become common, or mankind won't survive the next century."[4] And so Penn created a film in tribute to the spirit he found missing in American culture. The film, also titled *Into the Wild*, grossed about $18.5 million and was nominated for numerous awards, including two Academy Awards.[5]

How does the life of Christopher McCandless intersect with the life of Leonard Knight? Perhaps not at all in the historical sense. But on the level of myth—of stories that transcend historical fact and affirm and magnify greater cultural values—the two lives became intertwined. Krakauer's book recounts that McCandless traveled through Niland and Slab City on his great American adventure. And rolls of film found in McCandless's belongings after his death show that he saw Salvation Mountain, though we don't know anything about his experiences there, including whether or not he met Leonard Knight. It was not until the 2007 film *Into the Wild* came out that a *story* of the interaction between

McCandless and Leonard Knight appeared. That story, spanning less than three minutes of the film, has led thousands of pilgrims to visit Salvation Mountain.

What about those three minutes inspired so many individuals? The answer to that question lies in the mythic narratives into which both the book and the film tap. Both accounts embrace the romance of the American narratives of the West that suggest that true freedom comes outside of the boundaries of culture and society, in a place where one can experience nature and the *authentic* self. These same accounts suggest that it is in the West, maybe even especially in the Imperial Valley, which embodies so many paradoxical juxtapositions, that freedom and self are found. While the book celebrates the individual's journey into the wilderness in order to find self, the film focuses additionally on finding self in relation to others. The film attempts to tell both narratives and portrays Knight as someone who has achieved both—true freedom in the wilderness and a sense of self in relationship. Removed from the details of his own life history, Knight functions in the Christopher McCandless narratives as a fulfillment of the American dreams of the West and the wilderness; according to the film, Knight's life is a life *fulfilled in the wild.*

"I NOW WALK INTO THE WILD"

Even though McCandless died in the Alaskan wilderness, Krakauer crafted a narrative of his life that convinced many readers that he was a hero, a model for living. Krakauer attributed McCandless's death to "innocent mistakes" that "turned out to be pivotal and irreversible."[6] As a tragic ending to a story about searching for self, McCandless's death frames Krakauer's heroic narrative. It was simply a misstep on an otherwise beautiful journey into the wilderness in order to find himself. Demonstrating a courage of conviction and a desire to live outside social norms and laws, McCandless left behind a life of creature comforts and forged his own path in the world. Krakauer notes that McCandless's life represents larger trends in American narratives: "the grip wilderness has on the American imagination, the allure high-risk activities hold for young men of a certain mind, [and] the complicated, highly charged bond that exists between fathers and sons."[7] The book begins with a quotation from a postcard McCandless sent to his friend Wayne Westerberg on April 27, 1992: "Greetings from Fairbanks! This is the last you shall hear from me Wayne. . . . Please return all mail I receive to the sender. It might be a very long time before I return South. If this adventure proves fatal and you don't ever hear from me again I want you to know you're a great man. I now walk into the wild."[8] It seems even McCandless was wrapped up in the romance of his journey. For him, risk of life and limb was a demonstration of his commitment to finding freedom.

Born in 1968, McCandless grew up outside Washington, DC, in a well-to-do family. His parents, Walt and Billie McCandless, had two children together, Chris and Carine. On a trip to California in his teenage years, Chris McCandless learned that his father had previously been married to another woman with whom he had several children and to whom he was married when Chris was born. Learning this had a profound effect on Chris; he interpreted the information to mean that his whole life had been a lie, and he felt as though he could no longer live in a society that did not hold his father accountable for the choices he had made.

McCandless graduated with a high grade point average from Emory University in 1990, and after telling his parents of plans to attend Harvard Law School, he took off on his great American adventure. From his point of view, part of the adventure lay in renouncing the material goods that had kept him comfortable in his youth and had, from his perspective, corrupted his parents' lives. Before heading out, McCandless donated the $24,000 left in his educational fund to Oxfam so that it would go to feeding the world's homeless and hungry rather than to making his life so comfortable that he became complacent and simply accepted the American rat race as his destiny. The belief that he should not be tied to material goods only grew as McCandless continued on his journey. After his car broke down, he was emboldened, and "in a gesture that would have done both Thoreau and Tolstoy proud, he arranged all his paper currency in a pile on the sand—a pathetic little stack of ones and fives and twenties—and put a match to it."[9] His donation and burnt offerings symbolized his critique of the capitalist society to which he believed his parents and all Americans had become enslaved. As he gave up money,

McCandless felt less enslaved and able to more truly relate to other people and to himself. He was in search of authenticity and a true experience of the self.

His critique of capitalism intersected with his critique of governmental authority and the laws and rules that the government set up. In relation to both, McCandless wanted to set himself up "at the ragged margin of our society" so that he might develop a new set of personal experiences. He felt that his life was "none of the government's business." "Fuck their stupid rules," he declared to one driver who asked if he had a hunting license for the Alaskan wilderness.[10] McCandless claimed he lived according to higher laws—laws that did not derive their authority from corrupt institutions.

From his perspective, that distance from institutions—from capitalism, from his family, and from the larger society—allowed him the freedom to engage in a process of self-invention. In order to symbolize that shift away from his past identity, McCandless created a new name: "He was now Alexander Supertramp, master of his own destiny."[11] Perhaps because his new name sounded so incredibly invented, McCandless tended to introduce himself to people as Alex. That name provided him the anonymity that he needed to experience freedom. Because he had destroyed anything that would identify him as Christopher McCandless, it became very difficult for his parents to find him, even after hiring their own private investigator. Without those ties to the past, he could participate in one of the promises of the myth of the American West; he could be who he wanted to be, reinventing as he went. As master of his own destiny, McCandless had a very particular vision of what he wanted, summed up quite well in a passage from Tolstoy's "Family Happiness" that he had highlighted in his copy of the book: "I wanted movement and not a calm course of existence. I wanted excitement and anger and the chance to sacrifice myself for my love. I felt in myself a superabundance of energy which found no outlet in our quiet life."[12]

Part of his reinvention came in the new relationships he developed; his new identity was fluid in that it could be revised with each new encounter he had. Without a past that people knew, unless he decided to share it with them, McCandless could be many different things to many different people. He enjoyed the "intermittent company of other vagabonds he met along the way" with whom he could fashion new narratives and new philosophies of life. Jan Burres and her boyfriend, Bob, "rubber tramps" on the highways of California; Wayne Westerberg, who offered McCandless a job in South Dakota; and Russell Fritz (named Ron Franz in Krakauer's book and Penn's film), a retired and friendless widower who gave McCandless shelter and friendship in Southern California: all crafted friendships with "Alex." They were individuals on whom McCandless "made an indelible impression . . . most of whom spent only a few days in his company, a week or two at most."[13] These individuals remembered being moved by McCandless's charisma and inspired by his outlook on life and his courage to embrace an unknown future, to run toward it, in fact.

Perhaps nowhere is it clearer that McCandless profoundly shaped the lives of others during his journey of self-fulfillment than in his relationship to Fritz, who was eighty-two when he met McCandless. During their time together, McCandless learned leatherworking and the two bonded in countless conversations. In fact, Fritz taught McCandless how to make a belt, one on which McCandless etched the most memorable scenes of his journey:

> "ALEX is inscribed at the belt's left end; then the initials C. J. M. . . . frame a skull and crossbones. Across the strip of cowhide, one sees a rendering of a two-lane blacktop, a NO U-TURN sign, a thunderstorm producing a flash flood that engulfs a car, a hitchhiker's thumb, an eagle, the Sierra Nevada, salmon cavorting in the Pacific Ocean, the Pacific Coast Highway . . . the Rocky Mountains, Montana wheat fields, a South Dakota rattlesnake, Westerberg's house in Carthage, the Colorado River, a gale in the Gulf of California, a canoe beached beside a tent, Las Vegas, the initials T. C. D., Morro Bay, Astoria." The final thing inscribed on the belt is the letter "N," "presumably representing north."[14]

After McCandless left Fritz and headed north, he wrote a letter back:

> So many people live within unhappy circumstances and yet will not take the initiative to change their situation because they are

conditioned to a life of security, conformity, and conservatism, all of which may appear to give one peace of mind, but in reality nothing is more damaging to the adventurous spirit within a man than a secure future. . . . I fear you will follow this same inclination in the future and thus fail to discover all the wonderful things that God has placed around us to discover. Don't settle down and sit in one place. Move around, be nomadic, make each day a new horizon. . . . You are wrong if you think Joy emanates only or principally from human relationship. God has placed it all around us. It is in everything and anything we might experience. We just have to have the courage to turn against our habitual lifestyle and engage in unconventional living.[15]

McCandless's letter to Fritz represents a summary of his understanding of how to achieve fulfillment in this world. As he encouraged eighty-two-year-old Fritz to depart on his own similar journey, McCandless demonstrated how his life philosophy was developing: settling and staying equaled failure, secure futures meant spiritual death, and joy came in unconventional living, not necessarily relationships. McCandless bought into the mythology of freedom found in the American West and encouraged Fritz to "start seeing some of the great work that God has done here." He further instructed him to "pick up the hitchhikers, for they are generally good people and there is much to learn from them." Finally, he counseled him to take his journey "economy style": "No motels, do your own cooking, as a general rule spend as little as possible and you will enjoy it much more immensely."[16] Nowhere did McCandless more clearly link anticapitalism, freedom, and space than in this letter. That Fritz took McCandless seriously showed the extent to which the elder's life had been changed by the encounter. Fritz "placed his furniture and most of his other possessions in a storage locker, bought a GMC Duravan, and . . . occupied McCandless's old campsite."[17]

While the fact that McCandless had been shaped by his relationships—despite his insistence that they did not matter much—is clear in Krakauer's narrative, what is highlighted is his interaction with the western landscapes he encountered. In fact, Krakauer chose to name each chapter of his book after the place that serves as the setting for the narrative. This choice indicates that place is not only setting but also character in Krakauer's narrative. In the American Southwest, the desert "sharpened the sweet ache of his longing, amplified it, gave shape to it in sere geology and clean slant of light."[18] According to Krakauer, McCandless fell into the category of individuals who were ambivalent about human sexuality because they "embraced wilderness with single-minded passion." Perhaps so. McCandless, Krakauer writes, had a yearning that was "in a sense . . . too powerful to be quenched by human contact. McCandless may have been tempted . . . but it paled beside the prospect of rough congress with nature, with the cosmos itself."[19]

And so McCandless hitchhiked to Alaska and set off into the wild in order to find the freedom he sought. He wanted to commune with nature and the cosmos itself, and he found that communion in spaces. Inside the bus where hunters found McCandless's body, they also found a piece of plywood on which McCandless had etched these words:

> Two years he walks the earth, no phone, no pool, no pets, no cigarettes, ultimate freedom. An Extremist, an aesthetic voyager whose home is *the road*. Escaped from Atlanta. Thou shalt not return, 'cause "the west *is* the best." And now after two rambling years comes the final and greatest adventure. The climactic battle to kill the false being within and victoriously conclude the spiritual revolution. Then days and nights of freight trains and hitchhiking bring him to the great white north. No longer to be poisoned by civilization he flees, and walks alone upon the land to become *lost in the wild*. Alexander Supertramp, May 1992.[20]

For Krakauer, the fact that McCandless's "greatest adventure" led to his ultimate demise was a romantic wilderness tragedy. The popularity of Krakauer's version of McCandless's life was rooted in the fact that Krakauer was able to tap into long-told American narratives about an individual who left the trappings of civilization and went to *a place* that liberated him from society and from the self he had defined in relation to others. He went *into the wild* in order to discover who he truly was.

Krakauer was clearly taken by the romance of the long- and oft-told myth of the American frontiersman who went into the wilderness, struggled with all that was wild there, and through taming the wild became an independent man. I use "frontiersman" and "man" here intentionally. This myth was in no small part about American manhood. Even before the American Revolution, and more so during and after, European Americans were looking for something that made them distinct from their European counterparts. One element they saw as setting them apart was the seemingly endless land populated by indigenous peoples who also, like the land they populated, needed to be "tamed." Of course, this perspective was shaped by an ethnocentric, private property–oriented, Christian eye that only saw what was white and "civilized" as anything of value. It was in that context, though, that the story of the American hero— embodied in such fictional and nonfictional characters as Natty Bumppo, Buffalo Bill, Wild Bill Hickok, and Theodore Roosevelt—developed.

There were many generational iterations of the American hero wilderness narrative; its incidentals and descriptive aspects were clearly tied to the context in which they were written. At the same time, though, the core of this American myth remained the same: the hero left civilization and all of the wealth and status that he held there, and he left his social self behind as he went into the wilderness to find a new self. That self was found in the unbounded freedom of the wilderness, where he had to learn to rely on self rather than society. The struggle made him a man, the story went, and an *American*. More frequently than not, that story ended with the man returning to civilization, having learned the lessons of independence, democracy, self-reliance, and strength. He then offered those gifts back to the civilization he had left behind.

The romantic nature of this myth lent itself to readers finding Alexander Supertramp a tragic hero. He sought out what had beckoned Americans of so many generations, freedom in the wilderness. He went out to discover who he was away from the trappings of civilization and capitalism, which threatened to define and then crush his sense of self. He went into the wilderness to find himself—and he did—and he died in the endeavor. He never had a chance to return to teach others the lessons he had learned. He never had a chance to appreciate the gifts of his education. He learned his lesson as he was dying, alone in the wild. Krakauer's narrative reiterates this point over and over as it juxtaposes

McCandless's life with the life of countless other Americans who went into the wild to find self.

"THERE IS A PLEASURE IN THE PATHLESS WOODS"

So begins Sean Penn's cinematic rendition of McCandless's story based on McCandless's journals and Krakauer's book. Written and directed by Penn, the film starts with the text of a Lord Byron poem:

> There is a pleasure in the pathless woods;
> There is a rapture on the lonely shore;
> There is society, where none intrudes,
> By the deep sea, and music in its roar:
> I love not man the less, but nature more . . .

The poem is followed by the words Christopher McCandless wrote before he set off into the Alaskan wilderness from which he never returned: "I now walk into the wild." Though the book and film begin in similar ways, they do not share overarching messages. The nature of their differences explains the significance of the inclusion of Salvation Mountain and its importance to the cinematic narrative that is Penn's interpretation of McCandless's journey.

Although the book focuses on the places McCandless visited and the freedom he found in those places, the film highlights the psychological aspects of his story. Krakauer's text has the room to compare McCandless to other western adventurers, including Krakauer himself, arguing that McCandless fits an American "type." While the text makes these claims, the film focuses more on the relationships in McCandless's story. The film is about McCandless, his family, his friends, and his journey. Perhaps nowhere is this subtle distinction better highlighted than in the chapter titles used in the book and film. Krakauer chose place names for his chapters, highlighting the setting as a meaningful character in McCandless's journey: "The Alaska Interior," "Stampede Trail," "Carthage," "Bullhead City," "Anza Borrego," "Davis Gulch," "Fairbanks," and the "Stikine Ice Cap," among others, organize the story of McCandless's great American adventure. In the film version, segment titles highlight McCandless's internal developmental process: "My Own Birth" (not actually detailing McCandless's birth but the beginning of his journey), "Adolescence," "Manhood," "Family" (detailing his experiences with the chosen community he encountered in Southern California), and "Getting of Wisdom." These titles structure the film's narrative, making the film about relationships in a way that the text is not. Nowhere is this more emphasized than in Penn's choice to have the voice of McCandless's younger sister Carine, the family member to whom he felt closest, narrate her brother's journey. She discusses their past, his choices, and the impact those choices had on his biological family.

While the book painstakingly follows McCandless to each site in his narrative, the film focuses on two landscapes and highlights McCandless's experience in each: the glacial tundra of the Alaskan wilderness and the hot, stark Southern Californian deserts. The cinematography of the Alaskan wilderness communicates the magnitude of nature and the smallness of humanity in such great settings. McCandless thrills in this landscape, blazing hunting trails, shooting game, picking berries, and running with the caribou. He is enamored with its freedom. However, in that wilderness he is always alone. In the deserts of Southern California, McCandless also finds joy, joy that comes not only from the landscape but also from the communities he meets and the relationships he forms there.

The film spends a good bit of time detailing McCandless's experiences in Slab City, described by Krakauer as an "old navy air base that had been abandoned and razed, leaving a grid of empty concrete foundations scattered far and wide across the desert. Come November, as the weather turns cold across the rest of the country, some five thousand snowbirds and drifters and sundry vagabonds congregate in this otherworldly setting to live on the cheap under the sun."[21] As we have seen, inhabitants of the spot include retirees seeking out the warmth of the sun, ex-hippies, rubber tramps, and more. It is a potpourri of many walks of American life, and the inhabitants' attitude is perhaps best summed up in a song about the community, performed in the film: "We ain't got much money, but we got lots of class / If you don't like my style—kiss my ass."[22] In fact, the attitude of the inhabitants of Slab City generally resembles McCandless's: it is a critique of a strictly capitalist system and the laws that accompany that system. It is in Slab City that the film develops McCandless's relationship to Jan Burres, who serves as a mother figure to him, and he as a surrogate son to her. She encourages him to contact his parents and assures him that they are worried about how and where he is. It is also in Slab City, the film suggests, that McCandless cultivated a romantic relationship with a young woman called Tracy Tatro. McCandless does not have a sexual relationship with her, but he does provide her with a certain amount of wisdom as she gives him the gift of relationship. As they part, McCandless says to her, "Just remember that if you want something out of life, you've got to reach out and grab it."

Tatro is the character who invites McCandless to Salvation Mountain. There they meet Leonard Knight—played by himself in the film—who takes them on a tour of the mountain, just as he has for countless other visitors. While touring, McCandless asks Knight about his understanding of love:

> Knight: Everybody . . . in the whole world is loving me . . . and I want to have the wisdom to love them back.
> McCandless: You really believe in love then?
> Knight: Yeah . . . totally. . . . This is a love story that is staggering everybody in the whole world. That God really loves us a lot.

Inspired by Knight's words, McCandless and Tatro climb with Knight to the top of Salvation Mountain and look out over the surrounding oceanic desert landscape. "I really love it here," Knight tells them. "I think the freedom of this place is just so beautiful. . . . I'm contented here in the desert. . . . I'm living where I want to live." After hearing this from Knight, the three descend the mountain and Knight offers his visitors the opportunity to leave their handprints on the mountain. Their handprints seem to serve as witnesses to their presence, their togetherness, before they head off on different paths. They highlight touch and touching as a key component of experiencing the mountain, and they represent the human desire to leave a mark, to make a difference in the world. During this brief scene, the two visitors find an artist who has gone into the wild and found his place there. He is living in freedom, where he wants to live.

The scene is significant in the film. First, Knight stands out as the only character in the film, among countless seekers, who is happy *where he is*. He has found the freedom and satisfaction that the wilderness offers, the ability to live outside the capitalist system, and he has been able to stay there. Knight experiences not moments of freedom but an entire lifetime of it. It seems that this is precisely the reason that both Slab City and Salvation Mountain warrant a scene on the belt that McCandless makes with Fritz. According to the film, the two spots are remembered along with South Dakota, the Colorado River running through the Grand Canyon, and the Gulf of Mexico. The progression of scenes on the belt ends with an "N" for the northern Alaskan wilderness to which McCandless heads. The belt serves an important symbolic function in the film, as the record of McCandless's most joyous experiences in his western adventure, where the places teach him about communion with others and with the natural world. But it also marks McCandless's starvation in the Alaskan wilderness, where he must continuously bore new holes in the belt in order to have it fit him. While he created the belt of memories with a dear friend, the audience sees that McCandless marks his starvation alone.

Nowhere is the ultimate message of the film better communicated than in its focus on one of the final comments McCandless writes before he dies: "Happiness is only real when shared." In the film, his death is filled with visions of an open sky (suggesting his love of the natural world) and scenes of reunion with his family (demonstrating his need for community). Just as in the book, McCandless is a lone romantic hero, but that heroism is tempered by his recognition that he needs people in his life. The tragedy, then, is that this realization happens only when he is trapped and physically unable to return to a community. McCandless did indeed write "happiness is only real when shared" in the margins of *Doctor Zhivago* alongside the passage "And so it turned out that only a life similar to the life of those around us, merging with it without a ripple, is genuine life, and that an unshared happiness is not happiness. . . . And this was most vexing of all."[23]

The difference between the book and the film is that the film confirms McCandless's final comment by presenting his last hallucinations and visions as ones of family and community. Quite differently, Krakauer equivocates about the remark: "It is tempting to regard this latter notation as further evidence that McCandless's long, lonely sabbatical had changed him in some significant way. It can be interpreted to mean that he was ready, perhaps, to shed a little of the armor he wore around his heart, that upon returning to civilization, he intended to abandon the life of a solitary vagabond, stop running so hard from intimacy, and become a member of the human community." "But we will never know," ends Krakauer. In fact, Krakauer may be unconvinced because McCandless's final remark does not fit well with Krakauer's narrative. His narrative is of a man who finds himself alone in the wilderness, in his struggles with nature. That McCandless may have made an end-of-life change in his philosophy does not fit with the book's overarching message; that he died alone seeking to know himself in the wild does.

In only a few minutes of film time, Leonard Knight stands out as one of the film's heroes, as the perfect blend of an individual who has achieved freedom in the wilderness away from all of the trappings of society but still experiences the joy—and the love—of shared community. He is alone and not alone at the same time. Leonard Knight achieves what Christopher McCandless *and* Alexander Supertramp sought: happiness. And yet the film's portrayal may imply more similarity between Knight and McCandless than there is. Perhaps the difference is best summed up in the quotation that introduces this chapter: "To the desert go prophets and hermits; through deserts go pilgrims and exiles."

Leonard Knight made his life choices because of his understanding that he had a divine calling, that he was being commissioned by God for a certain purpose. That sense of calling compelled him to build a hot-air balloon, inspired him to construct a monument, and encouraged him to fashion the mountain again after he initially failed. Knight was in the desert permanently because he believed God put him there. He ended up in the desert on his search for God, and in the midst of that journey he became a prophet. He was in some sense both a prophet-in-community and a hermit-on-his-own. McCandless's story is a different one; he was both a pilgrim in search of a sacred sense of freedom and a self-in-exile, unable to live in his society. McCandless was a wanderer, searching for meaning down each road he trod. We will never know if the prophet ever met the exile, but the film version of their imagined encounter has made Salvation Mountain a popular destination today.

As a prophet, Knight espoused a message about the wrongheadedness of the social values of his time. His removal from the capitalist world of private property and into a world based on gift giving allowed him to critique the status quo of the culture in which he lived. By removing himself to the wilderness, Knight created a platform from which he could critique the culture in which he lived. The wilderness provided him that freedom. But he had to stay there. His was not a brief passage through the wilderness about which he then might write a book when he was done, as McCandless had planned. His was not a narrative of movement. Knight had to create a space in order to create a different way of living—it alone allowed him a genuine and sustained place of critique.

At the same time, it is important to note that Knight was not, despite all appearances, a hermit in the classic sense. Although Knight could not return to civilization the way the classic western narrative suggests, people could come to him. He was in community with the pilgrims and seekers who came to hear his message—they were his chosen community. He hardly knew them, and yet he had a love for them and with them that was a crucial aspect of his motivation. Yet we must remember that the community Knight created was quite different from most other communities. Knight felt a religious call to love everyone, but there were few people with whom he spent more than an afternoon. As each visitor arrived at Salvation Mountain, Knight told and retold the same stories. He heard other people's stories and often witnessed profound experiences that were shaped by the artwork he created, but that was the extent of most of his relationships—an intense afternoon of shared space and storytelling. Knight was a prophet and hermit at one and the same time. He was often surround by people and yet profoundly alone in the wilderness with his God.

He believed God gave him an artistic gift in order to communicate a message of love for humanity. According to Knight, God gave him the skills to create a space where he could live, thrive, and provide an alternative vision of the future. According to the film, Knight most assuredly knew what McCandless apparently learned on his own journey—that happiness is best shared. In the film, Knight serves as evidence of that claim; in his life, Knight demonstrated that the relationships between space and community are much more complex than the film suggests.

Motivated by the book and the film, thousands of pilgrims come to visit Salvation Mountain. By visiting Knight's world, they can easily participate in a portion of McCandless's journey. In their own journey to Salvation Mountain, rather than the Alaskan wilderness, they can realize and experience that while freedom may come in stepping outside the trappings of civilization, it may also be realized in community. In an afternoon, and from a prophet, they could hear the wisdom that McCandless spent years trying to find. They could enter into the philosophy of the American journey into the wilderness and learn wisdom from a prophet who had removed himself from the culture that values that freedom narrative. They could find freedom amid the paradoxes. Christopher McCandless's intense journeying caught the imagination of our culture through two interpreters and two interpretations, one captured in a book, the other in a film. His was a search for the true self and an authentic life, a struggle with which so many can empathize.

McCandless believed that the place to find authenticity was *somewhere else,* and he journeyed to the West to find those places. Through these narratives we can explore our own responses to the American West's paradox of freedom. And Sean Penn's film *Into the Wild* places at the heart of that paradox the figure of Leonard Knight and the image of Salvation Mountain—a paradox that has called thousands of pilgrims to drive hours off the beaten path, searching for that freedom and authenticity for themselves.

5

"Up Close, It Became the World"

Pilgrimage to Salvation Mountain

What is a pilgrimage? . . . A pilgrimage is a journey
undertaken in light of a story. A great event has happened;
the pilgrim hears the reports and goes in search of the evidence,
aspiring to be an eyewitness. The pilgrim seeks not only to confirm the
experience of others firsthand but to be changed by the experience. . . .
As they return to ordinary life the pilgrims must tell others what they
saw, recasting the story in their own terms.

—PAUL ELIE, *THE LIFE YOU SAVE MAY BE YOUR OWN*

It was like an Oprah moment or something . . .

—PILGRIM TO SALVATION MOUNTAIN

Up close, it became the world; a few steps away it began to resolve into
the puny production of a single human being."

—WILLIAM T. VOLLMAN ON SALVATION MOUNTAIN

"God is love" is today's mantra . . . and I *felt* it.

—PILGRIM TO SALVATION MOUNTAIN

THE FIRST RULE FOR most things in the desert is movement. In a world where dust devils rip through the landscape and then dissipate just as quickly as they begin, tumbleweeds stroll across a road, and bees migrate from crop to crop and then fly on to other climes, movement is a given. Most of the humans of the Imperial Valley mimic these movements, following the patterns of the natural world. Migrants from Mexico and Central America pass through on their journeys to find jobs in the Californian agricultural sector or in the state's cities. Retired snowbirds pass through to appreciate the warmth of the sun until it becomes *too* hot. Social dropouts who retired before they began a career and who love the romance of the open territory ride their bikes and hitchhike down the road. Tourists arrive to see the Salton Sea and Salvation Mountain and then continue on their journeys to Palm Springs resorts or the beaches of San Diego. Migration moves people in and out of the space. These people are often wanderers; they exchange first names and have no expectations that the friends or enemies they make one evening will be there the next day. Movement is the rule rather than the exception. Salvation Mountain's pilgrims travel from all over the region and the world to experience it, to hear its stories, and to *feel* its message.

In June 2011 I witnessed one pilgrim interact with the mountain on an experiential, sensory level. A nineteen-year-old woman came to visit Salvation Mountain because she had heard about it from a friend. She had not come all that far—her journey did not last more than a few hours—but her experience clearly transcended a distance that could be measured on any map. This young woman lives in Tijuana, Mexico, on the California border. Each weekday, she crosses the US-Mexican border to attend a community college in San Diego. Like Leonard Knight, she is a border crosser.

Her car slowed as she approached the mountain, taking it in from a distance. When she got out of her car, she tentatively looked around, waiting for affirmation that she could move around the space. Leonard Knight was there that day but wasn't feeling well. He was up for sitting under the tarp in the back of his broken-down, painted station wagon, but not for greeting people and walking them around. He asked me to explain to her that she could explore and take pictures wherever she wanted. She did. In fact, she moved slowly throughout the mountain, a contemplative look on her face. The time she spent moving through the space—climbing and touching—was about twice as long as the time most pilgrims spend.

When she was done, she came up to Knight, who was still sitting in the back of his station wagon surrounded by a few folding chairs for pilgrims who wished to join him. She thanked him and talked to him briefly, admiring his work. Then she asked if she could continue to sit with us. "Of course," Knight said. After about fifteen minutes of the three of us just sitting there in silence, Knight leaned over to her and said, "You know God loves you, right?" and she just started to cry silently. After a while she said, "I want to know that but I don't yet." And he replied, "God's here in the silence, so just sit with us and *feel* God." She did. After another twenty minutes or so, she stood up and thanked Knight again for creating a place where she could truly feel God. "You are always welcome here," Knight said. And she left.

What does this experience and the experiences of countless other pilgrims have to tell us about religious experience and activity? How can we understand the need to see, to touch, and to feel—impulses in Christianity that can be found in the gospel stories of the disciple Thomas, who doubted Christ's resurrection and insisted, "Unless I see the mark of the nails in his hands, and put my finger in the mark of the nails and my hand in his side, I will not believe"?[1] What can these experiences tell us about how people receive the anticonsumerist, antihierarchical gift world that Knight has tried to create in the middle of nowhere?

SENSATIONAL EXPERIENCES

Scholars of material religion have challenged academic discussions of religion for emphasizing belief over action, word over image, and thought over emotion. First, these dualistic categories are not easily imposed on actual religious lives. People live in the messiness of religion with little reflection on how they might separate belief and action or word and image. This is true even of Protestants, whose Reformation tradition declared sensory experiences of religion to be baser, emphasizing *the word* and *belief in the word* over anything else.

To complicate matters further, people do not always articulate religious experiences in terms of word and belief. Those experiences often remain in a category beyond full expression precisely because they are the most profound. Religious studies scholar David Morgan argues throughout his work that religious belief, even though we think of belief as an intellectual activity, is actually an embodied activity. "Making, exchanging, displaying, and using artifacts are principal aspects of human doing," he reminds us. Most religious peoples "live their religion in the grit and strain of a felt-life that embodies their relation to the divine as well as to one another. The transcendent does not come to them as pure light or sublime sensations in most cases, but in the odor of musty shrines or moldering robes or the pantry where they pray."[2] Religion resides in the self and the stuff, and the distinctions between the two are often not significant distinctions to the person experiencing it all. Belief does not always precede action. Rather, "people do what they want to believe," Morgan writes. "They make belief in the things they do."[3] This reminder is particularly pertinent to our discussion of pilgrimage to Salvation Mountain. Knight has "made belief" in making his mountain, and some pilgrims "do belief" in their journeys to the mountain and in the activities they participate in there. Pilgrims travel to a space they understand to be sacred in order to feel and experience the divine in profound ways. In that space they participate in an aesthetic, embodied engagement of Salvation Mountain's message.

Morgan has also challenged the way scholars of art and image tend to understand religious believers' interactions with sacred objects. He disputes the idea that sight is the primary sense and that it is primarily an intellectual sensory activity. He asserts that sight is often thought of as a "pristine and distant form of contemplation" and that we imagine it as disembodied and immaterial. He argues instead that we must think about sight in relation to other senses and that we must remember that seeing is an embodied activity. In talking about the embodied nature of sight, Morgan discusses embodiment in two separate yet interrelated ways. First, sight is part of being a body, and being seen is something humans experience as bodies. Second, sight is shaped by the social bodies in which we move.[4] To see "is to see for oneself, but also with others, and thereby to see with the eyes of a social body."[5] Our communities teach us how to see and what to see, what should be visible and invisible and how to interpret what our senses take in.

Morgan emphasizes the way that senses work together in order to create experience. In particular, he asserts that sight anticipates touch— by seeing "mass relative size, distance, movement, and texture." If seeing functions to anticipate what something will feel like, then "religious seeing would mean encountering the sacred in material terms." The senses work together, and the way that they work together is structured by that which they encounter in the world.[6] As we will see in the instance of Salvation Mountain, Knight constructed a world emphasizing *felt* religion. This should come as no surprise; Knight created the mountain in order to express his own profound experience of the divine. His experience began with a warming of his heart and then manifested itself in the material world as he tried to create a piece of artwork to honor his own embodied experience. When pilgrims come to Salvation Mountain, their senses often work together toward a tactile experience of its religious world view and claims about the divine.

In order to understand how pilgrims experience Salvation Mountain, we must examine how they experience it as embodied beings. Even before they arrive, many pilgrims experience Salvation Mountain as an image. They see it in the film *Into the Wild* (discussed in chapter 4) and they read about it online. Those online experiences may happen at the "official" Salvation Mountain website or in more informal interactions, such as when friends share their experiences and photographs of the mountain on social networking sites like Facebook. People experience Salvation Mountain in the online world. But is that experience anything like experiencing the actual place? Is clicking on images of the site the same as *being there*?

For some, it feels like it. Modern culture has so privileged vision over the other senses that it seems as though seeing online is the same as presence. What we see looks "real": "We cannot smell it, we cannot taste it, and often we cannot hear it, but what passes colloquially for 'virtuality' is a sole function of its visual representation."[7] Douglas E. Cowan argues that even though the online world may provide religious believers with important experiences, it does not, in the end, replace experiences of place because "we remain ineluctably embodied, ineluctably emplaced."[8] Visiting Salvation Mountain online engages only one sense. Perhaps this is the reason so many visitors to the actual place claim, "It's so different than what it looks like online," "I was imagining something different after I saw the pictures," and "It's much more and much bigger than I expected." When people experience Salvation Mountain online, they may well have a moving experience based on what they have seen, but do the images alone make it moving?

Those experiences are profoundly shaped by the history of the actual, offline location. How people have experienced Salvation Mountain, how they have written about it online, and how they have communicated it to their friends shape the way future visitors experience it. The social body ensures that future visitors' experiences are shaped by stories they have heard. These stories then structure new pilgrims' experience of the place.[9] And so the online world of reading stories and viewing pictures often serves as a first step in people's journey with and to Salvation Mountain. It is the first part of "you have to be here to really get it." The online experience is the work of the social body molding how people see and experience the mountain.

Is the experience of Salvation Mountain online the same as being there? Yes and no. Online images serve as visual invitations to experience the message and the mountain. Yet they do not account for the desert heat, the smell of paint, the feel of the mountain. At the same time, they may well provide the feeling that God has moved through Leonard Knight and that the mountain is what it claims to be. The privileging of the visual that happens online, merged with the stories of others' encounters with the actual mountain, may well cause an online viewer to *feel* Salvation Mountain and quite often encourage the viewer to go to the place. The invitation is understood. Some of those viewers travel to the mountain, leaving their homes to visit what they have come to understand as the sacred—to *touch it*—and to return home.

Those online stories and imagined communal worlds call thousands of people to Salvation Mountain each year. And the first sense that pilgrims put to work in their experience of the mountain as a *place* is vision.

Salvation Mountain is seen long before it is heard, smelled, or felt. A few people still stumble upon Salvation Mountain on their way to somewhere else, even though it is not on a well-trodden path and has not relied on stumble-upon-ers for its popularity. For most, however, Salvation Mountain is a destination. Perhaps one destination among many, but a destination no less. The mountain makes a promise to everyone who drives by it on the road. It is not the ordinary. It is not the everyday. It is strange. It is weird. Salvation Mountain promises to be *something else*. The sight of Salvation Mountain draws people to it. Vision is a promise. It is "a sense that oscillates between scanning and concentrated focus," David Morgan writes. "To see means skimming the surfaces of things in a broad range in search of what one wishes to hone in on and inspect more closely. When an image arrests our attention, we move close. Another way of saying this is that we look in order to behold, and behold with the prospect of holding."[10] Vision may invite, encourage, and promise touch, and this invitation is ever more significant in terms of religious artwork because it promises a material encounter with the immaterial divine realm. Most pilgrims' experiences of Salvation Mountain begin with sight, usually of images on the Internet. Those images invite them to visit the mountain and to experience it as embodied beings whose senses, they believe, may well better connect them with the divine. The ultimate promise is that of *feeling* in a spiritual sense, an embodied experience that transcends the senses and makes the beholder *know* the presence of the divine.

The vision of Salvation Mountain is, at first, just that. It is image. It is an assault on the colors and textures of the desert. One visitor explained that he was "not sure what to expect. When I got across the railroad tracks and began to turn the corner I saw the Mountain. It was truly breathtaking. 'God Is Love,' can be seen from far away."[11] Another pilgrim remembers quite clearly her approach to Salvation Mountain, an approach that began with a sense of feeling lost, which transitioned into disappointment and then emerged as awe as she came closer to the mountain and *saw* it. "'What mountain? It is a desert out here!' but I kept on driving. As I got closer, my nerves and fear started to set in, mind you; I was alone in a very odd location. I had passed several hitchhikers, dreadlocked hippies, campsites of leftover 'Flower Children' from the 60s, desert people, campers and seekers of the strange, like myself. . . . There it was, Salvation Mountain! I pulled over to the side of the road to park, and yes, somewhat in disbelief. My initial thought was 'You have got to be kidding; I drove out here for this?' I cannot express to you enough this is where first impressions can be so wrong! . . . As I walked closer, I found myself in complete and utter 'Awe.'"[12] This pilgrim traveled with expectations, expectations that were first disappointed and then met in spades. And they were met only as she came closer to the mountain and began to see it in a new way.

William T. Vollman, historian of the Imperial Valley and visitor to Salvation Mountain, described his experience in a similar way: "Up close, it became the world; a few steps away it began to resolve into the puny production of a single human being."[13] What was it that made these two visitors feel both unimpressed *and* full of wonder? Perhaps it was the scattered paint cans, the junk littering the area, or the mountain itself. The scale seems to inspire two types of responses in people, at times even in the same person. There is at one and the same time a "*This* is it?" response and a "How could one person do all *this*?" response. In part, it is hard for anyone to imagine what a thirty-year project will look like. Yet this strange juxtaposition captures something deeper that is occurring. From a distance, Salvation Mountain invites one to it because of its colorful landscape juxtaposed against miles of dusty-brown and sagebrush-green landscape. It does not seem large or mountain-like, though. It does not jut up from the earth in a particularly impressive way. Yet when one draws nearer and accepts the invitation to focus on all of its intricate details, and when one stands at its base and looks up, the mountain does indeed "become the world," filling the field of vision and dramatically altering the horizon. It is in the midst of these contradictory sensory experiences that pilgrims often experience a sense of awe.

David Morgan tells a story that speaks to this odd juxtaposition well. The story is about a Brazilian woman who had never heard a shofar but had always heard stories about it and anticipated the time when she would be able to participate in the experience of hearing it: "The first time I saw it, I was expecting a huge, majestic horn, something like the long horns of those cattle on the open range in Brazil. But when I saw the little sheep horn and then heard it, I was underwhelmed. 'This is the shofar?' I wanted to ask. Yet everyone around me became suddenly quiet and listened with absolute attention. Then I understood. It was a call to the tribe and they responded with complete silence."[14] In this story, the woman hears the sounds of a people, sounds that mark their peoplehood, and the response of that group is utter reverence, an acknowledgment of what binds them to one another.

It is the contradictions that call to people and invite them to step closer and to engage Salvation Mountain more fully. The sight of the mountain may invoke a sense of its insignificance, yet at the same time, the stories that people have told about it shape visitors' experiences and draw them closer. They have come all this way because someone has told them about the meaning of this place. Once they enter into the place, the symbols and the stories call them to attention, call them to a shared experience of peoplehood with others who have visited Salvation Mountain, a people with a prophet and a piece of art at their center.

It is only after approaching Salvation Mountain and with a little bit of focus that the words painted on it become central. From a distance, the central text is "God Is Love." The text itself *is* the vision. The word becomes image, already shattering a dualistic world view. "The aesthetics of the word as image has overtaken its literary content," writes Timothy K. Beal about other works similar to Knight's Salvation Mountain.[15] In the case of Salvation Mountain, the message and the words (the Word, in the biblical sense) as image merge. From a distance, all is sight. Up close, the words and the message become more complex. Up close, the contradictions and messiness of lived religion continue to overwhelm the senses.

That Knight dwelt in the space meant he burst through his society's understandings of private and public, desert and garden, sacred and profane. "It's no coincidence," writes Beal, "that most of these roadside religious spectacles are also private homes. In one sense, this is simply a practical matter. . . . But I think there's more to it than that. What is home, after all? An extension of myself, a shelter from the storm, a piece of private property, a locus of intimacy and secrets."[16] Beal explains that this shattering of the boundary between the public and the private is rooted in a desire to express to others the depth of personal religious experience. Knight, then, allowed people a boundaryless home to walk into and experience. That invitation into the depth of his experience is disarming to visitors. Beal claims that "it's an invitation to relationship, with me or anyone who visits."[17] By constructing a sacred, storied space and choosing to dwell in it for all the world to see—by living in a place where nothing is private, including his own most profound religious experiences—Leonard Knight broke through conventional boundaries. In so doing, he invited visitors into his home to witness his ultimately inexpressible experience.

The first place visitors usually enter is what Knight calls the "museum," the cave-like set of structures attached to the mountain. In the museum, visitors see all sorts of found art—car doors, car windows, tractor tires. They also see pictures of the mountain in its various phases, miniatures of the mountain, awards Knight has won, and photographs of him with different people. All of these items one might expect to find in a family room, on a mantel, or in the center of a home. And visitors seem to understand it this way. One woman described that her favorite part of the experience "was the tiny room with all the preserved pictures in it—of the different stages of the mountain, of Leonard. It made me realize the mountain and those who helped him with it were his family who he loved as such."[18] Another visitor claimed that the "most meaningful part for me [was] the small rooms filled with knickknacks/personal items because they brought me a sense of nostalgia."[19] Those small rooms made Knight into a kindred spirit who preserved memorabilia and photographs of important moments in his life like anyone else. He might be a prophet, a hermit, a desert father, and a bit crazy, but these homey traits showed that he was human. The private side confirmed his humanity, that he was "just like us" even when he was profoundly not. These personal items scattered throughout such an astoundingly public space are evidence that the artist was a man with profound relationships, even though he spent most of his time telling the same story over and over again to new strangers. In starting tours in his family room, where people could see his mantel, Knight disarmed and invited them into a relationship from the very beginning of their experience of Salvation Mountain.

For many pilgrims, after seeing, the next sense engaged is hearing. Perhaps most important to the site's sacred status is that pilgrims hear the stories that called Knight to the place and kept him there. But they also hear the desert. "The silence was eerie," described one pilgrim. "Nothing but the howl of wind and the flapping of old rags." They hear the silence, and in the silence that distinguishes this place from the places where they live, they hear the stories that explain the space and how Knight understood it. The stories they hear and the evidence they then see explains to them how this space was holy for at least one individual. Stories shape this world. "In fact," David Morgan writes, "a world is an unstable edifice that generations constantly labor to build, raze, rebuild, and redesign. To use a literary metaphor, a world is a story that is told and retold in order to fortify its spell of enchantment. And there is never just one story, never just one world. Worlds collide with one another as well as contain within themselves the contradictions and disjunctures that must be mediated or concealed for the sake of a world's endurance."[20] From Leonard Knight, pilgrims heard how the space became a *place*. They heard how the man became an *artist*. They heard his *prophetic speech*. And they felt their role; they understood their responsibilities as witnesses.

At the same time, what pilgrims see becomes more complicated. They see the details of the mountain, the work that was put into it. They read the text, noticing the details of the verses that discuss God's love, that explain how God acts in the world. They begin to see the details of Knight's Christian message. They piece together what they are witnessing as they hear the stories about the experience that created the words and image. Morgan explains that the power of images "consists in their ability as extended forms of embodiment to provide the touch and hold of what they (re)present. That is why we feel so sure about what we see. We code it with the feelings that are important to us and we (be)hold what appears . . . as if it were a kind of footing or touchstone or way marker."[21] Religious pilgrims focus on particular aspects of the mountain and then the mountain serves as a concrete embodiment of what they believe to be true, that God is love and is working in the world or that Jesus wants to enter into their hearts. The promise becomes more concrete. It declares: you are a witness.

That witness then develops in the sense of touch. The mountain serves as its own witness—viewers can't *see* what happened to Leonard Knight so many years ago, but the mountain can feel like a concrete message of the truthfulness of Knight's claims. Climbing the mountain means climbing thirty years of effort for a particular set of beliefs. What Leonard Knight *knew* in his body the day he became a born-again Christian he *lived* for the next thirty years, constructing a place that communicated, as well as he could, that feeling. Knight attempted to embody an embodied experience. Walking on the mountain is an experience in itself. Pilgrims experience the mountain as embodied beings. Even the mountain is a changing, living, embodied being. The mountain changes and is changed.

The mountain serves as evidence that precedes words and expressed emotions. It is the experience and the emotion itself. That the mountain exists in the middle of nowhere contributes, for those who believe, to the factual claims it makes. In this regard the narrative is the same: only a crazy man would spend thirty years in the desert, *unless* that crazy man was sent there by divine command. David Morgan argues, "What goes into our experience and evaluation of a material object . . . its weight, texture, size, shape, and color . . . also its relationship to other objects and its placement in the space we ourselves may inhabit next to it. . . . All of these qualities of a thing . . . bear directly on its physical connection to our bodies. This suggests that a thing is, in part, what it offers us physically— pleasure, pain, or threat of harm. Already we see that a thing is more than a thing, more than itself."[22] Salvation Mountain's location challenges its status as simply roadside religion; it seems to indicate that it is beyond the realm of a money seeker creating religious kitsch. The location itself indicates to believers the truthfulness of Knight's claim.

Pilgrims respond. They receive Knight's message as embodied beings and follow the patterns and actions of those who have come before.[23] Pilgrims to the mountain often note that being able to climb the mountain serves as a means to a deeper level of *feeling* the mountain's message. They use such words and phrases as "unique," "mind boggling," and "welcoming" in their efforts to articulate what it means to them to be able to climb Knight's witness to God's love. One woman visiting from Germany claimed that "climbing the mountain [was] like being a part of it. It's like the heart in the desert."[24]

In these examples it becomes clear that touch is a central component of the religious experience of Salvation Mountain, both physical touching and being "touched" in the sense of being "moved by." These two types of being touched are related in intriguing ways. There is the touch of a physical body against another body or object, as when visitors to Salvation Mountain place their hands on the mountain, climb the mountain, and feel the material reality of it. Then there is the sense that they have *felt* the truthfulness of the mountain's claims about God. Religious believers have at times called this feeling a sixth sense, an internal movement or conviction that they might describe as being touched by the Holy Spirit. That internal sense is often caused by the physical act of touching something one believes to be sacred.

Both types of touching—the sensory and the internal—occur frequently in pilgrim narratives. This is not surprising. Knight's most intense experience of the divine came through a warming of his heart, feeling touched by the spirit, and then seeing and hearing the ways the intense experiences of *feeling* manifested in his life.[25] That he would then create an artwork that invites pilgrims to engage all of their senses but to ultimately focus on *feeling* makes sense. His mountain is a witness that can be seen, smelled, felt, and touched, asking its visitors to serve as witnesses and to *feel* in their own right.

Though sight often precedes touch in experience, there is a crucial distinction that helps to explain why touching the mountain often surfaces as the central sensory experience for pilgrims. When we see something, we maintain the distinction between the viewer and what is viewed, the self and the other. There is me and there is the object that I am looking at. In this way, sight can reinforce a dualistic perspective. Touch, however, troubles such dualisms. When I touch something, my hand conforms to the shape of it. My body is affected by its interaction with whatever I touch. Similarly, my touch can transform the object that I am touching. Thus the relationship between self and other, between me and the thing I am touching, becomes more complicated. Self and other, subject and object are two more dualisms Salvation Mountain collapses. For this reason, touch can often surface as the most profound aspect of a religious experience.

Climbing the mountain is a distinct way of touching and feeling that surfaces again and again in pilgrim accounts. "He encouraged me to climb . . . especially with that camera," one pilgrim recounted:

So I half climbed and half crawled up the sunshine-yellow stairs and foot path that wind across the face of the mountain. My backpack shifted alarmingly and I put my hand down for support. I noticed in places that the paint had chipped off in great thick chunks and I wondered how many years of dedication and how many layers of acrylic it takes to produce something like that. As I climbed I tried not to think about safety measures and building codes and I was quite relieved upon finally reaching the top. Slab City lay quietly to the east, a field of tiny white boxes. To the west, the sparkling Salton Sea. A giant cross made of what appeared to be telephone poles cast a shadow hundreds of feet long across the dirt. Below me, the creator of the crumbling beast squinted through the sunlight. He was smiling at me, delighted. Looking down at him, I couldn't decide if the man was crazy or brilliant. Then I realized that I was the one who had just spent the afternoon climbing to the top of a giant art installation in the middle of the desert.[26]

Perspective changes as one climbs, as this narrative so clearly recounts. The bodily experience of being disoriented and righting herself, of shifting her vision from the immediacy of the mountain's paint, to the horizon of the Salton Sea, to the shadow of the cross, all affect the way she *sees* things. No longer is Knight the crazy one, or if he is, she is too. If he is brilliant, then she is too. A shift in her perspective changes the way she sees the world, affirming Knight's mission of building the mountain to encourage visitors to change their perspective and to *feel*. His grin is a welcoming one, and one that demonstrates that he knows the perspectival shifts of thought she is experiencing. In fact, he may have even planned it that way.

Throughout much of the academic discussion about the senses, touch has been denigrated, seen as one of the baser senses. But a few twentieth- and twenty-first-century theorists have argued that touch is the way that we most deeply experience the world. Our body, our flesh, "implicates the self in a world of contact, proximity, and intimacy. . . . The world is experienced because it is intimately touched, a process that renders tactility more than merely a sense."[27] For one visitor to Salvation Mountain, the most important touch was a feeling in her heart: "As a spiritual person, a believer, but very private about my religion, my beliefs, and not one to ever preach to anyone . . . as one who has visited and prayed in some of the most historical and ancient churches still standing, I must say this modern-day monument touched my heart without a doubt."[28] Touching becomes a way of making the mountain and the experience it attempts to articulate *really real*. Touching is a means toward an embodied experience of beliefs. It affirms the beliefs, allowing the expectations of the mountain and the experience of the mountain to unite.

Touch is an interesting sensory experience to explore. It troubles the easy dualisms that some of our senses may reinforce. It also is a sense that is highly regulated in our culture. We are told from our youth, perhaps especially in our youth, not to touch certain things. The things that we aren't supposed to touch are especially important, we are told. A common phrase repeated to children and to some adults is "you see with your eyes, not with your hands." What does this saying imply? That to truly behold something, our impulse is often to actually hold it. Touching makes sight more powerful; it confirms what we see. One of the many sets of things we are told we should not dare to touch is art. We are to behold it, but not to hold it. We are to be moved by it, but through our eyes. Knight's mountain crashes through those cultural regulations. He built a piece of art that invites viewers to climb, to experience it. In so doing, he asked visitors to transgress the boundaries their culture upholds. They transgress boundaries as they climb a mountain of transgressed boundaries. Knight asked them to behold it and to hold it.

Pilgrims also experience Salvation Mountain through the embodied activity of helping to paint it. For years Knight invited people to help him paint the large art installation that needs at least two coats of paint each year just to survive the desert storms. After Knight became ill in 2011, and even four or five years before then, after he slowed down in his work on the mountain, more and more of the painting was done by others. This activity, for some, serves as an act of devotion to the God that the mountain celebrates. Pilgrims come and paint so that the mountain may continue on into the future as a testament to the love of God.

PRACTICING PILGRIMAGE

In contemplating the impact of Salvation Mountain on its visitors, it is important to consider the part the senses play. But how does pilgrimage to the mountain fit into established and more formal definitions of pilgrimage? What is pilgrimage? For Victor and Edith Turner, anthropologists who defined the field of pilgrimage studies, pilgrimage is about leaving the world of the everyday and journeying to touch the sacred. The point of pilgrimage, they note, is to "get out, go forth, to a far holy place approved by all." The Turners claim that over the course of the journey, pilgrims shed their social identities and bond with other pilgrims in an egalitarian, liminal community. It is in this liminal world, in which social distinctions are rendered meaningless and the pilgrim's identity is defined by her or his status as pilgrim, that "the tainted social persona may be cleansed and renewed." Pilgrims enter into a world of "anti-structure." The journey itself—which must be away from the average and the everyday of social status and hierarchy—allows this to happen. Over the course of the journey, pilgrims enter into a "new, deeper level of existence."[29] They then return to the average and the everyday with a new sense of religious purpose.

The Turners' primary argument about what happens over the course of a pilgrimage, published in 1978, has been critiqued, though it has largely withstood the test of time. Coleman and Eade argue that it has simultaneously "proved immensely resonant" and "run the risk of taking studies of pilgrimage down a theoretical cul-de-sac, both in its all-encompassing character and in its implication that such travel could somehow (or at least should ideally) be divorced from more everyday . . . processes."[30] This second point is a significant one, especially relative to Salvation Mountain. The Turners argue that pilgrims leave behind the everyday world and enter a unique and entirely separate space and time where they can shed their everyday selves. It is not that simple.

As pilgrims visit Salvation Mountain, they do not, in fact, shed their identities. Knight may claim that those identities do not matter—he does not ask what pilgrims do for a living—yet car, clothing, hairstyle, and many other symbolic indicators communicate class and social status. Knight may not have cared about those things, but that does not mean that they vanished. Pilgrims continue to be who they are in the world, even though they may well experience Salvation Mountain as a world where their social identity is deemphasized.

Further critiques of the Turners suggest that pilgrims do not experience sacred sites in uniform ways. At a site, pilgrims do not all agree about what happens—what they see, smell, hear, and touch. Instead, they interpret as individuals, precisely because of their social locations.[31] Multiple interpretations are a given at pilgrimage sites. At the same time, the makers of sacred space, individuals such as Leonard Knight, shape the space in the hopes of encouraging a particular experience. Sacred spaces are organized around an imagined map of the place. They "allow for different routes to be taken and can be interpreted variously by those who move through them, but they also orientate travelers in ways which the latter cannot entirely control."[32]

Knight's sacred space, then, offers a map of his alternate world with a marked path. One is invited to see, then hear, then touch, then feel. After hearing the stories of how the mountain came into existence, pilgrims enter the museum, personalizing the mountain in a specific way. It was Knight's family room, his home, a window into his soul. The mountain that pilgrims climb next seems to serve as evidence of who he was and what he believed. This path, at least, is the way Leonard Knight wanted pilgrims to experience the place. The range of pilgrims' stories and experiences evidences the multiplicity of their experiences.

This chapter begins with a quotation from Paul Elie about how "pilgrimage is a journey undertaken in light of a story."[33] Pilgrimage is a particular type of activity. Indeed, it is movement from point A to point B and back, but it is movement with intention and with the anticipation that point B is somehow different from point A, somehow special. Pilgrimage "requires an attitude of reverence toward the site one visits." A comparison with tourism might illuminate what makes the activity of pilgrimage distinct. In his study of sacred space, Lawrence Hoffman writes, "Tourists visit sacred places with the epitome of Martin Buber's I-It attitude, in that place is a thing to be appropriated for one's own use. They will even rearrange the scenery to take the best picture of it." Even though tourism has always been a part of pilgrimage—pilgrims have to eat and sleep somewhere, after all—pilgrims take a different approach to their movement and the space that they inhabit: "Pilgrims view their journey's end with the attitude of I-Thou. To them the sacred place is alive, imbued with its own character, resonant with a message regarding the metaphysical nature of reality itself."[34] This expectation—that the space is sacred and resonates with part of a larger reality—often aligns with the promises that Salvation Mountain makes. Vision and expectation unite so that pilgrims often leave satisfied, thinking that they have seen something amazing even if they do not believe that they have seen a manifestation of the sacred. They recognize Salvation Mountain as a place set apart.

Those who come for religious reasons come because they see in Salvation Mountain a message that they believe American society—even the entire world—needs. "It's the highest way I have ever seen that someone lives in and with God's love," claimed one pilgrim. "The contrast between the desert and the mountain shows the contrast between a life without God and a life with God."[35] This sense that Knight lived apart and had some special knowledge of the divine because of that gives his message an aura of truthfulness to believers. They expect God to be there when they arrive, and they encounter their God in the man and the mountain. "I believe that 'god' is love, not some being in the sky," claimed one pilgrim. "It's nice to see it in such a bold statement."[36] "God is love" is the phrase most repeated throughout pilgrim accounts. It is the message that Knight highlighted in his storytelling and on his mountain, and it is the message that the majority of religious pilgrims take away. Still others take away a message about what can be achieved when a life is so focused, so dedicated to one message. All of these messages satisfied Knight. They communicated to him that that his mountain was doing precisely what it was supposed to do.

Pilgrims tend to *feel* something, a commitment, a passion, God's love, or some indefinable combination of all three. "It really feels like God has his hand in this place [and it] has lots of messages from God."[37] One person recounted that coming to the mountain was "as if I came to see an old friend." Another that it was "overwhelming, in a good way . . . hard for your mouth [not to] drop open."[38] Sharing their experiences minutes after they had them, pilgrims claim that Salvation Mountain is familiar, filled with love, and welcoming. They feel at home. Knight offered them an "I-Thou" relationship, one in which he saw the beauty in every person (because he believed God does), and he wanted to interact with everybody on a personal level because of it.

RETURNING TO POINT A—AND TALKING ABOUT POINT B

In the narrative of pilgrimage, the return to everyday life is important. What one takes back, how Point B gets injected into Point A, tells us a great deal about the meaning of pilgrimage to a particular pilgrim. How an individual recasts her or his own narrative, how she or he owns it, individualizes the pilgrimage narrative and hints at the ways that sacred sites are organized to inspire particular responses. Paul Elie writes that as pilgrims "return to ordinary life the pilgrims must tell others what they saw, recasting the story in their own terms."[39] After reading countless Salvation Mountain pilgrimage stories, several types of pilgrim narratives emerge. An example of one such narrative, Knight inspiring passion in the pilgrim, is evident in the story of Clara Hung:

> During my visit at Salvation Mountain, I realized how much passion Leonard Knight has and made it a point to continue his ongoing legacy through my own life. I do not follow any religion, but seeing the mountain, I understood how God's influence was enough to give someone a purpose in life. I left with an important message that I learned from visiting Salvation Mountain, which was that I am capable of reaching all of my dreams. I carried this experience to my life at home by furthering my productivity. Rather than just attending school and working a part-time job, I understand that there are so many opportunities out there for me. Naturally, I used this newly discovered knowledge and have started to pave my way to accomplishing

my dreams. If it weren't for my visit to Salvation Mountain, I may never have started working as a photographer for a well-known website, donating the profit of my art work to a church, raising considerable amounts of money for charity, or many other endeavors that I have become involved with. I learned that taking my interests to the highest level capable is integral to leading a life of movement that has not been experienced before. My visit to Salvation Mountain has transformed me into a much more positive person with an optimistic outlook on everything. . . . I doubt that the effect I received from my visit I will ever feel again. Yet, the inspiration of Salvation Mountain is enough to let me move forward with my life with a creative and prolific future that I desire.[40]

For Hung, the passion and the single-minded dedication to a vision of the future was the message she took from Salvation Mountain. She read her own life and its commitments over and against Knight's and rededicated herself to a new vision of her own future. Her narrative clearly demonstrates that she sees her current success coming from her stick-to-itiveness and optimism, traits she saw in Knight and injected into her own life. For Hung, Knight's welcome to the mountain was an invitation to dedicate her own life to her own passions. His life served as inspiration, an inspiration to move forward. She returned to her life with a renewed commitment.

Another common theme in pilgrims' stories is that of feeling a divine spirit in the place, a theme expressed in Cindy Holleman's account:

It all started when I was a child approximately 8 years old. Although we live in a desert, my mom and dad liked to go camping in the desert. . . . Each time we would go camping to the east it would include a trip to the mountain. I don't really remember Leonard at that time but I remember my dad would take paint and explain Leonard's mission to me. I saw it literally grow over the years. I remember as a small child the mountain only being a little more than the size of a big-rig. Then each year or every other year or so it grew. During my early 20s I went to college in San Diego and I didn't get to the mountain or camping much but I never forgot the message. When I had a child we started going to the mountain infrequently but I wanted her to see what Leonard had created over the years. It still continued to grow the times we took her there. About 4 years ago, my church group was looking for a field trip and we went to the mountain. This is when I met the man I had only heard about for my entire life! It was like an Oprah moment or something. Truly, God filled the space we were in when Leonard was talking about all the years he'd been there, how the mountain (and now the surrounding creations) were built and mostly to remember "Keep it Simple, God is Great and he loves us." My now 17-year-old daughter felt a real kinship with Leonard. . . . Like I said—it's kind of a short but sweet story but it's my story and I can only hope that everyone gets to connect with Leonard before he leaves us.[41]

Holleman's narrative stands out for a number of reasons while also tapping into common themes that run throughout pilgrim stories. Unlike single-visit pilgrims, Holleman has seen the mountain evolve over decades, has witnessed how Knight's dedication has played out over the course of several years. Before she knew what the mountain was, she knew that it was a work in progress, a life's love. She saw the evidence of Knight's message, an aspect that is so important to so many pilgrims, evolve. Salvation Mountain became a familial place, and Knight a point of reference in her family's constellation of narratives. They understood who they were as religious people and as family members in terms of how they connected to the ongoing evolution of Salvation Mountain. Part of the family's narrative merged with the narratives of Salvation Mountain and the family's connection with the holy there. Because of this intersection of stories in her life, Cindy felt the spirit in the place. For Holleman, God was present and surrounding her at each moment. And that kind of presence continued in the life of her daughter. Holleman's constellation became her daughter's, and thus Knight showed the spirit to another generation of her family.

For some, the artist plays the most significant role in their recasting of the story. Patrick Rea, a filmmaker who has chosen to create a film narrative about Knight, describes the desert father this way:

Leonard is an enigma. First he is paradoxical: He is a loner yet
receives more visitors than maybe anyone in the world. He is a failure
in every way the world measures a man; yet he has developed engineering innovation with adobe that has never been observed by
archeologists. . . . He is a high school dropout; yet on a given day can
say some of the most profound, convicting, and relevant things I've
heard anyone say. . . . I have come to realize that all of Leonard's
shortcomings are actually by design, as no one else could have done
what Leonard has done. . . . From the middle of the most Godfor-
saken place on earth, Leonard has shared his testimony. . . . The simple fact of the matter is, there is no one like Leonard. He has been one
of the men in my life that has taught me how to be a Christian. . . . I
truly believe, "He is the greatest story that has never been told."[42]

For Rea, Knight serves as a model of Christian life. He recognizes that
by all conventional standards, Knight would come up as a loser in
American society. And yet, as Rea sees it, he was not. In fact, he succeeded
by a different set of standards, one Rea locates in the Christian tradition.
Knight's version of what a Christian should look like is one that he wants
to follow. For him, Christianity is witnessing, standing apart from the
things society values, and sharing a testimony. Knight's testimony informs
Rea's.

These three stories demonstrate different messages that pilgrims
carry away from Salvation Mountain. Knight may have organized the
space in a particular way, a way that attempts to elicit a specific type of
experience, but the pilgrims tap into the stories in their own individualized way. Their individualized narratives are not all that different from
one another, but they highlight different facets of Knight's life, his message, and their experiences. Pilgrims' expectations affect their experiences. Their lives and their approach to the site shape their way as much
as Knight's intentions for their experiences do. All told, those who visit
Knight's mountain, who are either open to spiritual messages or committed to Christian ones, seem to have their ideals confirmed. Knight's
mountain—away from all of the standards and expectations of American
culture—represents an idealized world where spirit rather than money

rules experience. But what they describe again and again is a *felt* spirit, one that's embodied, one that dwells in relationships and in place. Even more than seeing the sacred, touching the sacred forms the center of their narratives. As one pilgrim wrote after her first visit to Salvation Mountain, "'God is love' is today's mantra . . . and I *felt* it."

6

"Lord Jesus,
I Gave Them My Very Best"

Bad Religion, Bad Art, and the
Quest for Good Taste

A little bad taste is like a nice dash of paprika.

—DOROTHY PARKER

Whatever you do, it mustn't be kitsch.

—ROGER SCRUTON

SINCE 1982 POPULAR AUTHOR Sue Grafton has been writing
stories about private investigator Kinsey Millhone. Each one of her mys-
teries, *A Is for Alibi, B Is for Burglar, C Is for Corpse,* and on down the
alphabet, follows Millhone through a series of antics that usually winds
up with her catching the bad guy. When Millhone introduces herself to
the reader, she describes herself as having "hazel eyes, a nose that's been
busted twice, but still manages to function pretty well I think. If I were
asked to rate my looks on a scale of one to ten, I wouldn't. I have to say,
however, that I seldom wear makeup, so whatever I look like first thing
in the morning at least remains consistent as the day wears on." This
sassy, funny, and intelligent main character keeps readers coming back
again and again to find out what mystery she will solve next.

In 1990 *G Is for Gumshoe* appeared in bookstores everywhere. Its setting was none other than Slab City, Salvation Mountain's next-door neighbor, where Millhone encountered a number of social outcasts and odd folks. As Millhone is headed to the Slabs for the first time, she passes Salvation Mountain without going in. "In the distance, to the right, I caught sight of a hillock of raw dirt, crowned by an outcropping of rock painted with religious sentiments," she says. "GOD IS LOVE and REPENT loomed large. Whatever was written under it, I couldn't read. Probably a Bible quote. There was a dilapidated truck parked nearby with a wooden house built on the back, also painted with exhortations of some fundamentalist sort."[1] Grafton doesn't get Salvation Mountain quite right— neither the makeup of the mountain nor the sentiment of its artist—but in describing the space, she links the oddity of Salvation Mountain to the oddity of the Slabs and its inhabitants. These people don't act like the rest of us do. These places aren't like the places that we are used to, she implies. They are odd. They are strange.

"Odd," "strange," "weird," and "eccentric" are all terms that have been used to describe Knight and Salvation Mountain. And there should be no wonder. Leonard Knight celebrated and expressed his religion in ways most people in our culture would be embarrassed about. He gave us *big* religion, and his "mountainload of the lord's word" is in the middle of the desert and covered in thousands of gallons of paint. How do we *look* at it?

What we must consider is that terms like "weird" and "wacko" are matters of perspective; they ultimately lie in the eye of the beholder. Over the course of our lifetimes we are taught what to see, what not to see, and how to see, and the words we use to describe what we see are contextual, socially and historically located. What seems weird and strange to one culture or person may be considered holy and beautiful to another. For one person, the strange is the key to unlocking the holy, while for another the strange is tied to the profane. We look at Knight's mountain and see what our culture has taught us to see. Good and bad, shocking and mundane are tied to the context in which art is viewed rather than to traits inherent to the artwork.[2]

Through social cues and pressure we are taught by our culture what "proper" taste looks like. Just as we learn manners, values, and social norms, we grow up learning how to be in the world and how to look at the world. We are judged and socially punished when our tastes veer too far off the beaten path. We are socially rewarded when we "get it right." Race, class, gender, and education all play a role in defining what "normal" tastes look like. There is a wide range of tastes in American culture because each person has been taught taste and had choices structured by her or his specific cultural location. In part, our culture accepts us as "adults" when we have internalized social expectations and tastes to the extent that we become our own judges.

Taste is something that we learn from the institutions and power structures that define our cultures. And because taste is structured by institutions, it can serve to reinforce power structures. Using the work of theorist Pierre Bourdieu, Marita Sturken and Lisa Cartwright argue that "taste may often work to the detriment of people of lower classes because it relegates objects and ways of seeing associated with their lifestyles" to a status deemed "less worthy of attention and respect."[3] As we will see, these forces operate to shape the way some individuals see and respond to Knight's mountain and to Knight himself. Artistic taste is very much tied to how the viewer has been trained to see the world, and taste extends beyond the artistic to all aspects of life.

What we will see is that the artistic critiques of Salvation Mountain parallel the religious ones. We are trained by our culture to not only appreciate and discern what is art but also appreciate and discern what proper religion is and is not. When we see it, we *know* whether it is good, bad, authentic, or faked, even though we are not always conscious of how we know. In the case of Salvation Mountain, we can see the parallel claims of taste: bad art and bad religion are often overlapping accusations.

At the same time that there are people who would critique Salvation Mountain and find it lacking in artistic and religious merit, there are those who seek out the strange and weird, those who embrace what the culture deems unworthy of "good taste" and are drawn to places like Salvation Mountain precisely because it transgresses the boundaries of what good art and good religion are supposed to look like. These seekers make up a portion of Salvation Mountain's visitors. They do not come to see or have religious experiences. They do not see the site as holy or sacred in a religious sense, though they may see it as special because it is art. These visitors are drawn to the kitsch, to the weird, to what makes Salvation Mountain both "outsider art" and "outsider religion." These seekers of the strange can also teach us about how society reinforces expectations about taste precisely because they intentionally want to thumb their noses at social expectations. They glory in the weird and drive hundreds of miles out of the way to see it in order to reinforce their own understanding of their identity as people who reject the cultures and tastes of the mainstream.

What Leonard Knight intended for pilgrims to see, what he intended them to believe as they walked away from Salvation Mountain, may or may not intersect with how they receive the mountain. Class, race, education, gender, and social location, *who we are*, contribute to what we see. It is thus the issue of taste—both artistic and religious—that we must consider.

NOT EVEN ART?

Like any art that straddles the boundaries of what is deemed culturally and artistically acceptable and unacceptable, Knight's work has withstood some controversy. The status of the site as a sacred one has been contested precisely because of its boundary transgressions. As discussed earlier, Chidester and Linenthal, in their study of American sacred spaces, have argued that sacred space is contested space. Though controversy has not played a large or consistent role in making Salvation Mountain sacred in the eyes of pilgrims, there has been some. And controversy makes for great stories.

It is not accidental that two of Knight's favorite stories to tell were, first, of his experience of being born again (the "beginning" of Knight's story because it launched him into a new phase of his life) and, second, of his experience of triumphing over the State of California when it attempted to declare Salvation Mountain a toxic dump and his artwork a pile of junk. It is a truly western story of the struggle between a "squatter" who developed the land and a "big government" that wanted to destroy what he built with his own two hands. The David-versus-Goliath narrative of conflict confirms the site's status as sacred to many listeners; it suggests that there are "evil" forces in the world attempting to profane Salvation Mountain by declaring it is not what it claims to be. In the end, those attempts reinforce the idea that the site is sacred because there is the possibility of its being profaned.[4] Knight loved the story of his battle with the State of California precisely because it confirmed the sacred status of the land on which he had built his life and his art.

Because Knight built his art on government-owned land, it came under investigation in 1994, when California attempted to develop a pay-camping site at Slab City. The state's experts declared that soil samples had "uncovered a high level of lead at Salvation Mountain, the result of Knight slathering it with an estimated 10,000 gallons of paint." In June of that year, the commission meeting in Sacramento "immediately agreed to spend up to $225,000 to clean up Salvation Mountain and the rest of Slab City."[5] Knight recalled that "it started when five or six pickup trucks came in, and they were hazardous waste experts, and they dug twelve holes in the mountain. Before the soil was even analyzed, signs were put up designating the area as 'hazardous.' . . . All of a sudden the papers started saying 'hazardous nightmare' and I was contaminating the area, and the man has to be stopped, and the mountain's a mess."[6] Critics jumped on the bandwagon, declaring that art may well have to be sacrificed in order to protect the environment. One such critic, Larry Bickman of Thousand Oaks, California, wrote in a letter to the editor, "How are painting and sand and, in effect, letting 100,000 gallons of pollutants into the ground water to be considered art? I guess if I dump some paint down my sewer drain and it flows to the ocean and discolors the sand, water, or swimmers then that is considered art too."[7] In this instance, Knight's detractors didn't define the mountain as *bad art*, but they denied that the mountain was artwork at all in order to suggest that there was no obstacle to tearing it down. In these narratives, the mountain became toxic junk profaning the sacred status of the pure environment.

In response to the editorialists, Knight wrote a song:

I contaminated California with a four-inch hand paintbrush
All I ever wanted to do was be an artist
Lord Jesus, I gave them my very best
California is going to hang me tomorrow
And put my body to rest.[8]

Knight's song, which he willingly sang to anyone who asked, portrays him as a rebel going up against a state that would deny his land's status as sacred and his own identity as both prophet and artist. The suggestion that a paintbrush could contaminate something as large as the geographical state of California shows how Knight understood his own place in the world. He was the "little guy" who went up against the big bully state government because he had God on his side.

After hearing that the state soil samples confirmed that the land had been compromised by the paint, Knight's supporters hired their own set of independent soil testers, who came to very different conclusions. In the end, Knight was able to prove that the mountain was not as toxic as the state had declared. But the story did not end there. Knight's supporters continued to come to his defense. The Folk Art Society of America declared the mountain a piece of art worthy of preservation and protection, putting Knight's work in the same category as Simon Rodia's Watts Towers in Los Angeles and Howard Finster's Paradise Garden in Georgia.[9] Later Senator Barbara Boxer of California entered a statement into the 2002 *Congressional Record*: "Leonard Knight's artwork is a national treasure, a singular sculpture wrought from the desert by a modest, single-minded man. It is a sculpture for the ages—profoundly strange and beautifully accessible."[10] Here Boxer claimed, with congressional authority, that Salvation Mountain was not only art but good art, worthy of being seen, protected, appreciated, and preserved.

Knight's experience with the controversy—the initial declarations that his mountain was a "toxic dump" and the later congressional statement that his work was a "national treasure"—served as evidence to him of divine support for his work. His understanding of the Boxer statement was that it placed him on par with one other piece of artwork. He happily told visitors that "Mt. Rushmore is number one and I'm number two. That's all there is. Now, how in the world did that happen?"[11] Knight was also heartened because he believed that the declaration that his work was a national treasure would protect it long after he was gone: "The exact word that kept Mt. Rushmore—a national treasure—is the same word that I've got, 'National Treasure.' Wow! I mean that's the same. So whatever Congress wants to do to keep it like it is . . . [is fine with me]. I'm praying a lot about that, because there are way too many people who would like to grab it."[12]

In the narrative of Knight's conflict with the state we can see just how intertwined judgments about what makes for "good" art and religion can be. While Knight understood the story through a religious lens, as an affirmation that Salvation Mountain was indeed a sacred space, Boxer and others affirmed the mountain's status as artwork. By doing so, they protected it, making it "sacred" in a different way. We surely cannot imagine bulldozers tearing through the Mona Lisa precisely because it is a treasured work of art. By declaring that the mountain was noteworthy artwork, they maintained the site's inviolability. Continued efforts to celebrate Knight's work culturally affirm his status as an artist and the work of his hands as artwork. Rebecca Hoffberger, of Baltimore's American Visionary Art Museum, also became a fan of Knight's and described his work as beginning with "love based participation."[13] Hoffberger and the museum worked to have the remaining pieces of Knight's hot-air balloon transported to Baltimore, where a replica of the balloon was constructed and remains on permanent exhibit.

When Leonard Knight built a monument to his God, he confirmed for himself the reality of his experience of the divine. After he completed the mountain, part of Knight's energies went toward ensuring that the mountain would outlive him. Knight understood Boxer's statements and his appearance in the film version of *Into the Wild* as divine and human confirmation that the site was precisely what he said it was, religious artwork.[14] Knight went through a lengthy process of attempting to canonize the mountain to protect its inviolability long after his death. He wanted others to agree that the site represented what he *knew* were good art and good religion. Each successful step in the process became a legitimization of Knight's accuracy about the site's sacred status—he read them as signs of success against the profane, secular forces in the society that he fled and a confirmation of his status as a prophet and an artist.

KITSCH, BAD ART, AND SENTIMENTALITY

Over the years, I have heard several people claim that Salvation Mountain is bad art and the work of an amateur. A colleague of mine once asked me how I could take Salvation Mountain seriously when it was so obviously the work of a wacko. That colleague also derided the people who visit Salvation Mountain; he claimed they were seeking some sort of fake religious experience and declared that the mountain was cheap art and kitsch. Exploring these dismissive comments and what they mean will help us to see and understand some of the critics of Salvation Mountain, those who see Knight as childlike, his work as overly sentimental, and his mountain as bad art.

"Kitsch," "kitschish," and "kitschy" are all terms that have been used to describe Knight's mountain and much religious art. What is kitsch? As a term its origins are not entirely clear. It came into popular international usage in the 1930s but may have been used several decades earlier by German painters. *Kitschen* is a German term that "has the sense of 'to collect rubbish from the street' and in the Mecklenburg dialect *verkitchen* meant 'to make cheap.'" In 1939 Clement Greenberg helped popularize the term in American circles with an article published in the *Partisan Review* in which he argued that "Western culture simultaneously produces both the abstract art of the avant-garde and the popular commercial kitsch of the 'rearguard.' . . . [Kitsch] is a debased copy of genuine culture that operates through formula, vicarious experience, and faked sensations." For Greenberg, there was a progression that led to the creation of kitsch: what started out as great art created by artists such as Picasso or Van Gogh was then "'looted' and 'watered down' only to be 'served up as kitsch.'"[15] A general definition of kitsch would be a work of art that is popular but that does not have any actual artistic merit, art that is not in good taste but is popular simply because it plays upon the baser emotions of the masses, particularly sentimentality.

Art historians and art critics have continued to argue that kitsch is imitation that "tries to be art but . . . fails. Kitsch lacks creativity, style, imagination, and nuance."[16] Gillo Dorfles, in his edited volume of essays titled *Kitsch: The World of Bad Taste*, exemplifies this position when he writes that the "element of falseness appears everywhere [in kitsch] . . . love, grief, birth and death are transformed into superficial emotions or hedonistic witticisms."[17] In the same volume, Hermann Brock claims that kitsch is "based on imitation and uses set recipes, is rational even when the result seems to be extremely irrational, or even positively absurd. . . . [It is] obliged to copy art in all its specific features . . . [and it therefore has a] lack of imagination."[18]

Religious kitsch takes special knocks from these same scholars. Dorfles writes that a majority, if not all, of religious art is kitsch because "it is usually aimed at a public who, it is thought, ought to be fed with inferior products rather than with products of any artistic merit."[19] Karl Pawek furthers this discussion by claiming that "when you consider what a high percentage of the population—judging by the windows of shops selling furniture, lamps, wallpapers and china—live in tasteless surroundings, it is not surprising that the religious pictures and objects which Christians have on show are also tasteless."[20]

Claims like the above demonstrate the perspectival nature of art and kitsch. Not many religious persons—not anyone, really—would call themselves tasteless, irrational, or absurd. Yet critics feel confident in making such claims about other people. They characterize what they do and what they value as art—thought-provoking high culture that inspires society to greatness. They draw on the authority of education, class, and training to make such claims. "Kitsch" they reserve as a term to describe that which inspires emotions and is low culture—*that which they do not want to see.* That which offends their senses. Kitsch is what *other people* like. By suggesting that they simply do not "get" kitsch, they distance themselves from the people and emotions they associate with it.

For precisely that reason, kitsch is discussed in dualistic terms. The concept of taste implies that poor taste, its opposite, exists as well. In an article titled "On Kitsch and Sentimentality," philosopher Robert C. Solomon discusses taste and what he calls "sweet kitsch," a concept that is important for understanding accusations that Knight's mountain is kitsch and bad art. Sweet kitsch "appeals unsubtly and unapologetically to the softer, 'sweeter' sentiments"; it is "often mentioned as [a] paradigm . . . of bad art." What critics hate most about sweet kitsch is its sentimentality; it promotes the "baser" and "softer" emotions of love, kindness, and sweet-ness—all emotions deemed less worthy by critics. And there is much of religious art that fits into this category. "Saccharine religious art (as long as it is serious and not sarcastic)" is sweet kitsch.[21] According to this narrative, sweet kitsch is something no "real artist" could stand to look at, let alone create.

Solomon offers several popular arguments critics use to suggest that a piece of art is kitsch. All of these arguments address the emotions the piece is supposed to evoke in the viewer and are worth exploring. One argument made about the artist and his artwork is that they "are *self-indulgent* and interfere with 'appropriate' behavior." This perspective asserts that kitsch has the power to distort "our perceptions and interfere with rational thought and an adequate understanding of the world." Other arguments deal with the effect kitsch has on the viewer. Critics claim that it promotes "*excessive* or *immature* expressions of emotion." Kitsch also attempts to "*manipulate* our emotions" or "evoke '*false*' or '*faked*' emotions," which, according to these critics, are "'*cheap*' or '*easy*' or '*superficial*.'"[22]

Solomon makes an important observation in his discussion of charges that a work of art is kitsch: the charges tell us more about the critic, her identity, and how it is related to her understanding of "taste" than they do about the artist, the actual piece of art, or any of its other viewers. The declaration that a piece is kitsch has much to do with the critic claiming a particular identity for herself. That does not mean that her feelings are not genuine. Solomon argues that the "unsophisticated viewer displays unselfconscious affection, not affectation, and the sophisticated viewer, with his or her mixture of embarrassed emotion and corrective disgust, is certainly not 'faking' that despised emotion." And so, whether officially trained or untrained, viewers are authentically responding to artwork. However, their cultural locations can lead them to entirely different conclusions.

When a critic claims that a piece of art is unsophisticated or "childlike," she is distancing herself from the creator and any appreciative viewers. Claims of sophistication, rationality, and maturity are functions of class and education. The critic implies that sophisticated folk do not have the emotions, particularly a public display of the emotions, identified with kitsch and, in particular, sweet kitsch. A Western narrative of intellectual development supports this distancing effect. In that narrative, faith is "equated with intellectual simplicity that diminishes in the course of gaining knowledge." Someone with a strong faith is equated with a child, someone who hasn't seen enough of the world or read enough books to realize that her beliefs in God are as ridiculous as belief in Santa or the tooth fairy. Even though the loss of faith may be painful, the "story justifies that loss; in it we tell ourselves that it was necessary to lose faith in order to advance in knowledge."[23] In the end, becoming an adult and having maturity and intellect are equated with the loss of faith, with seeing the world with eyes open.

At the beginning of this chapter I mentioned that in order to be considered an adult in a culture, one must internalize the tastes and norms of that culture and self-police based on those standards. Here we see a set of assumptions at work. Faith is associated with being a child, while rationality and reason (and a lack of faith) are tied to adulthood. Someone like Leonard Knight, who had the gall to reject standards about art and religious beliefs, is deemed childlike. There is a large chasm between the critic's argument that Salvation Mountain is childlike and Knight's claim that it is.

Knight wholeheartedly embraced the idea that he had a childlike faith. For Knight, the claim enforced his position as a true believer—he came to his religious faith uneducated and untrained and embraced the simple message that he thought churches and their educated leaders had forgotten. Matthew 19:4 confirmed for Knight his belief that coming to faith as a child was exactly what Jesus wanted: "Suffer little children, and forbid them not, to come unto me: for of such is the kingdom of heaven" (KJV). Whereas Leonard Knight saw childlike faith as the marker of a true believer, critics do not use the term as a compliment. Rather, "childlike" defines the emotions and theology surrounding the mountain as uninspired and simplistic. The baser emotions are those that are not only associated with the uneducated lower classes but also tend to be gendered female and associated with children. In this instance, "childlike" might be more aptly read as "childish."

Knight's mountain was created to invoke the emotion of love—love for God and love for humankind. It does not emphasize a theology of divine retribution, and it does not attempt to stimulate profound theological questions or discussions. Although it does not ask questions, it has its answer: love. In this way, it does precisely what sweet kitsch is supposed to do. It stimulates "the 'soft' sentiments of kindness and sympathy and the calm passions of delight." It is this trait, among others, that categorizes it as kitsch in the eyes of art critics. For them, "the best emotions seem to be the worst emotions where art is concerned, and 'better shocking or sour than sweet,' has become something of a rule of thumb for artists and a criterion of good taste for connoisseurs."[24] To charge that a piece of art is sentimental is to "say that it is very bad art—if, indeed, it deserves recognition as art at all—and to cast suspicion on both its creator and its appreciative audience."[25] Knight's emphasis on divine love and love of neighbor may well be what inspires believers to go back out into the world and be better people. It may be that seeing a Salvation Mountain magnet on the refrigerator reminds someone of Knight's simplistic reminder to *just love* family, friends, and God. Or Knight's mountain might inspire critics to see his work as simplistic and superficial, lacking the depth of other "higher" and ultimately more "rational" emotions. For these individuals, Salvation Mountain may well be the epitome of sentimentality and bad art. That there are magnets and puzzles that picture the mountain and that the mountain has been reproduced on a mass scale may serve as further evidence to critics that the mountain should make any sophisticated viewer nauseous.

BAD ART, BAD RELIGION

Even though lay Christians have used material objects and religious artwork to enhance their religious practices and beliefs throughout the history of Christianity, there has nonetheless been a long-standing tradition of disdain for material aspects of the faith. This disdain is rooted in particular biblical interpretations and a dualistic Cartesian world view. Undergirding this disdain is an interpretation of the second commandment, which condemns the making of idols: "You shall not make for yourself an idol, whether in the form of anything that is in heaven above, or that is on the earth beneath, or that is in the water under the earth."[26] Many Christians have interpreted this passage to mean that the use of images and artwork of any type is dangerously close to idol worship. Even more broadly, the passage implies to some readers that the material world itself, and the use of it to spatially and materially express religious ideas, is sinful and wrong.[27]

A dualistic world view has reigned throughout much of Christian history. As discussed in previous chapters, this world view separates the universe into either/or, black/white, good/bad dualisms with no room for nuances or gray areas. It begins with the classic dualism between God and humanity—who are imaged as wholly distinct from one another. The dualistic world view celebrates the supernatural, soul, spirit, intellect, and reason while denigrating the natural, the material, the body, and emotion. These classic distinctions have also been read onto social relationships. For example, men have traditionally been associated with God and intellect while women, the "second sex," are tied to the natural world and the body. This dualistic perspective shapes how believers see the material world: the sacred and the profane, what is of God and what clearly is not.

Though this dualistic world view is deeply rooted in Christian history, it runs against many of the foundational tenets of the Christian tradition. After all, one of Christianity's central claims is that God became human and lived among us. The idea of the incarnation, the embodiment of divinity, is not the only core Christian doctrine where we see the intermingling of the spiritual and the physical. The ritual of the Eucharist celebrates the body and the blood that, according to much Christian doctrine, offered a spiritual sort of salvation. This too is accompanied by a radical claim that a life after death is possible for the faithful and that it will be an embodied life.

Even though those central claims trouble a dualistic world view, Christianity has been profoundly shaped by dualisms. This dualistic approach is apparent, too, in the Protestant critique of Catholicism during and after the Reformation. Among many other criticisms of the Roman Catholic Church, the Protestant reformers argued that Christianity had become a tradition too focused on the senses. In churches of the day, believers would hear bells ringing, smell incense, participate in the Eucharist, and see images of Christ, Mary, and the saints. The Protestant reformers wanted to strip the altars and return Christianity to what they believed was its core: the Word. They attempted to remove sensory experiences during worship in order to focus the minds and hearts of believers on Scripture; *sola*

Scriptura, Scripture alone, was one of their rallying cries. These thinkers viewed believers who used "objects or images in their devotional lives or who [felt] that certain places [were] imbued with special powers . . . as needing spiritual helps or crutches."[28]

That same disdain for material manifestations of religious belief appeared also in disdain for embodied experiences of religion. This critique also intersects with charges that have been made against Knight and his mountain. Not only are material, artistic representations of faith suspect, but so too are embodied manifestations of spiritual faith. In the discourse against embodied religious experiences—experiences like Knight's, in which he claims the Holy Spirit entered his body, took over, and made him speak in tongues—we can see again that the charges often tell us more about the observer than the observed.

Accusations against religious "enthusiasm" (a term often used by critics to describe embodied religious experiences that aren't considered proper or in good taste) abound in American Protestant religious discussions. These accusations take place within religious denominations and between religious denominations; at their core lies the question of how God interacts with humans in today's world. Religious believers like Knight, who have had an embodied experience, explain that experience in religious terms. After all, Knight *knew*, in an embodied way, that the Holy Spirit enters into the physical realm. Yet the opponents of Knight and others, those who *know* that *this simply does not happen* or that *it does not happen this way* or that *it does not happen to this person*, must find a way to explain those experiences differently. These critics tend to use naturalistic language to explain what they believe are false experiences. That person over there, they claim, was deluded, has psychological problems, and does not understand how God really works in the world. "Most people associated true religion with order," writes religious historian Ann Taves, "and false religion, especially enthusiasm, with disorder."[29]

In religious discourse these accusations are often much more than religious claims. Claims against religious enthusiasm are often claims that the individual experiencing God in an embodied way is *not* of the same class, education level, race, or gender of the observer. To say that an individual is deluded, is convinced that God speaks to her when God does not, is to say that she is unable to tell the difference. In this instance, the "I" who knows that this is not a genuine religious experience is celebrated as rational and educated and the individual being observed has opened herself up to theological misinterpretations and bad theology. Thus experiential religion is deemed a religion of the heart (and all of the baser, nonrational emotions), while the religion of the viewer is deemed a religion of the head (and all of the implications of rational thinking entailed in that claim). The experience is, from the perspective of the observer, *bad religion*.

It is not only the childlike outsider-art nature of Knight's Salvation Mountain that has inspired charges that it is bad art but also the religious nature of the mountain. His art *and* his religion are open to such charges, and we see the intersection of the claims that Knight's mountain is both bad art and bad religion. For some viewers, including those who want to see Salvation Mountain bulldozed, this mountain represents a material, public manifestation of a distasteful, personal experience. These folks call it kitsch and bad art—nothing worth seeing. Some go so far as to declare the mountain a trash heap, likening it to something that truly offends the senses. In these charges they are preferencing what they understand to be the hallmarks of good taste: rationality, refinement, and encounters with the world through the intellect. In calling Salvation Mountain kitsch or bad art or bad religion, the critic is telling us about his or her own understanding of what taste and its opposite—bad taste—look like. In the critique, they are imbued with out-of-control emotion and embodied experiences of the world.

SEEKERS OF THE STRANGE

There are yet others who are drawn to Salvation Mountain precisely because it embodies what the culture deems strange and weird. These viewers embrace their status as outsiders to the establishments and institutions of good taste. They deny the authority of the educated elite to determine what is "good." They see in Knight a kindred outsider spirit who has thumbed his nose at the culture's rules and expectations and built his own artwork, which is an expression of what he believes to be beautiful. When they visit Salvation Mountain and appreciate its weird representations of the human condition, they choose to align themselves with Knight as individuals who stand outside the culture and critique the powers of the center.

One quiet afternoon in the summer of 2009, I was sitting with Knight at the base of Salvation Mountain when one such group arrived. Knight and I were in the midst of a discussion about the projects he planned to take care of in the cooler hours of the next morning. He pointed out to me the various shrubs jutting up through the cracks in the mountain. Some he wanted to keep—they were part of the artwork—and some he wanted to prune. Only he could tell the difference.

As we were talking, three vans pulled into the lot and about fifteen people piled out. They looked as though they had been cooped inside for some time. Most of the visitors in the group were in their early twenties, but an older couple, both professors, came over to Knight to explain that the group had road-tripped from an art school in San Francisco in order to study Knight's artwork. The professors explained that they had always admired Knight as someone who didn't just "break the mold" but didn't even care that a mold had ever existed. They called Knight a rule breaker, someone they truly admired for creating art that pleased him rather than creating art for others. They wanted their students to see this type of art so that the students could develop new standards and allow their creativity to flow. They asked Knight if he minded if the class stayed for the rest of the day to study his work in the hopes that the students would be inspired. An excited Knight agreed.

Immediately the students started to unpack the vans. Some had sketchbooks, some had easels, some had cameras and tripods. In spurts they would come over to Knight to chat with him about his artwork and then head off to contemplate the mountain. Knight loved the experience. The students commented on the details of the mountain, asked him about the process, and respectfully listened to his stories. After the group had been there for about two hours, two young women walked up to Knight to ask a question. "We're not just art students," they said, "we're also models. We'd like to pose nude on the mountain and were wondering if you would want us to stay in the museum or if it is okay with you if we pose on the face of the mountain." Knight stared at them. "You'd like to do what?" he said. "We'd like to pose nude," they said. "There's only one rule out here," Knight replied. "No one is naked on the mountain."

I'd never known such a rule existed; perhaps Knight didn't either until the words came out if his mouth. After the women walked away, Knight turned to me and explained that naked pictures taken at the mountain would focus people on the nakedness and not on the mountain's message. I didn't want to tell him that the message was clearly not their focus. They were there to study him as an artistic rule breaker and had just come up against his one and only rule.

I ended up speaking for some time with the professors and a few of the students. They admired Knight's message and focused some of their attention on the love at its center, but they were there, had traveled a long distance, to see the art that broke the rules. They were there to see the weird and the beautiful. How do those who visit Salvation Mountain for its weirdness describe their experiences? Why do they come?

In part, the visitors to Salvation Mountain who come to see a strange piece of art created by an odd man with a singular vision are attracted to that singularity of vision. At the same time, visitors are attracted to what is weird because it stands outside cultural expectations. By relishing in the weird, visitors can claim a distance from the centers of power and establish a position of authenticity and originality for themselves. "I don't follow the tastes or standards of my culture," they suggest. "Instead I flock to the weird and strange, embracing it and my own originality." Or as art students might explain, "I don't have to go to the Louvre to study great art; I can be challenged in my creativity in the middle-of-nowhere desert." Some of these visitors may have seen Salvation Mountain in *Into the Wild* and appreciate its outsider status from that medium. Or they may have seen it on Huell Howser's *California Gold* episode. Or they may have read about it in the book *Weird California*.

Part of a series that explores the "weird" in every state of the union, *Weird California* puts Salvation Mountain in the category of personalized property. Its authors write that it was particularly hard to discern what would and would not make the cut for California's weirdest places because the state "has always had more than its fair share of eccentric folks. Would you really expect them to live out their lives in cookie-cutter suburban houses? Not likely!" Instead the authors depict Knight and his fellow weird homemakers as creating space that is a "canvas on which to express their innermost personality to the outside world." These same artists are portrayed as molding their environments to "better suit their needs and aesthetic sensibilities."[30] Here the aesthetic is recognized as a key component of what sets these figures and the spaces they've created apart from the mundane and the everyday. And it is true that Knight's life's work satisfied his aesthetic desires—when he looked at the mountain, he saw a thing of beauty.

Knight merits a few pages in the tome, and the authors describe Salvation Mountain in this way: "Imagine if you will, '60s pop artist Peter Max erecting a mountainload of the lord's word in the middle of the Southern California desert, and you'll have an idea of what Leonard Knight's Salvation Mountain looks like." They recognize the fact that Knight's work juxtaposes images and texts that are not often placed together: "Flowers and waterfalls, American flags and hearts are artistically married to passages from the Bible and simple messages of joy, peace, and goodness." Here the authors point to some of the attraction of the mountain to seekers of the strange. Images and text that are not usually seen together, that we might not imagine as belonging together, are playfully connected at the mountain. Take, for example, the "Jesus Fire" portion of the mountain seen on page 31. In this small section of the mountain, a powerful theological concept for Pentecostals, "Jesus Fire," is surrounded by bright flowers in whimsical colors. The weightiness of the theology is offset and at the same time highlighted by the juxtaposition.

After explaining that Knight's work has some connection to his religious world view, the authors promise that "Leonard is well aware that some people will miss the spiritual significance he intended, but he is happy to have visitors enjoy his mountain any way they can."[31] Promising these same seekers that they will not have the religious message forced on them seems particularly important in this context. It recalls a comment that I heard many times when I chatted with visitors to the mountain—those who were interested in the mountain as art were worried that they would be meeting a missionary with a zealous faith. But the combination of the message of universality and inclusivism and Knight's welcoming personality, which was "not pushy or preachy," drew these visitors in. One noted, "The fact that he doesn't force his religion on visitors is my favorite part—it makes it very comfortable."[32] These folks appreciated that Knight was not about "'fire and brimstone' judgment" but "all about preaching God's love."[33]

Some of these viewers come because they were inspired by seeing Salvation Mountain portrayed in books or films, while others hear about it through word of mouth, both in the online and offline worlds. One online reviewer admired many of the same things about Salvation Mountain that religious visitors do: "I thought I needed to see it. I had no idea I needed to FEEL it. . . . What I can't explain to you . . . is the feeling you will have when you see this unique destination. You feel like you have left the world for a short time. It makes you envious of the people who have the courage to live in Slab City, and abandon the hustle-and-bustle of everyday life."[34] Here the visitor noted that the mountain was a space set apart, one with a different vision than the world surrounding it. The visitor then romanticized the vision as something that people often long for—an escape from everyday life.

While these visitors come in order to see this outsider artist's work, they often focus their appreciation on Knight's originality. They come because they enjoy American folk art or religious art. Many also note his reuse of materials as part of what makes him so admirable. Knight's mountain appeals to those who see the value of reusing the "junk" that society casts off. Several visitors commented that Knight was recycling: "All found objects, recycled and reused!"[35] Another called the mountain "just about the best use of what is available to create a divine scenario."[36] That recycled, discarded junk becomes part of a piece of art, a "divine scenario," impresses them. Here we see a total reversal of the comments made when the state tried to dispose of Salvation Mountain. Whereas in the first instance Knight's mountain moved from being called art to the denigrated status of trash, these seekers of the strange see power in Knight's transformation of his culture's trash into something artistic and beautiful. They herald this as a hallmark of his critique of the wastefulness of the culture he lives in. Some connect it to the mountain's anticapitalist message that they also treasure, its critique of American materialism.

Visitors may come simply because they see the mountain as "wacky business."[37] They appreciate that the work is "totally mad—painting on dirt . . . a cross between something from the Wizard of Oz and Alice in Wonderland."[38] Or they may see it as a place that "alternated between viewing what seemed like an artistic junkyard, to being transported back in time to some hippie retreat whose occupants had painted the area while under the influence of LSD." These folks often want to be clear that they did not come for any religious reasons. One woman in her twenties stated, "Well, I'm still an atheist . . . [but] the scale of this is pretty awesome."[39] Another young woman from Southern California claimed, "I feel I approached the Mountain with an artistic perspective, not a religious one, but [I] still picked up on and felt moved by the overall message."[40]

In addition to being drawn to the alternate world offered at Salvation Mountain, visitors also appreciate the ways that Knight has challenged the dualisms of the culture in which he lives. They see the intermixture of the natural and unnatural and of art and junk as setting apart the artwork from the rest of the world. And so the narratives told by the seekers of the strange have some resonances with the narratives told by religious pilgrims.

Untrained as an artist and as a theologian, Knight's material expression of his religious experiences can be troubling. Critics assume that because the mountain is painted in festive, Disneyland colors that it is only supposed to be given the degree of attention paid to all things Disney. And these critics make their accusation from an authentic place. Salvation Mountain does not look like the art they are used to seeing, and Knight's religious world view doesn't match up with how they understand proper religious experiences. That people might flock to see Salvation Mountain baffles them. Knight may have given his very best, but for them, that very best looks much like a colorful pile of junk.

7

The Disappearance of Sacred Space?

Authority and Authenticity in the Desert

Among the tortures and devastations of life is this then—our friends
are not able to finish their stories.

—VIRGINIA WOOLF

IN LATE 2011 LEONARD Knight entered a nursing home in El
Cajon, California, after facing heart failure and increasing deterioration
of his sight and hearing. Over the previous year, he had experienced several episodes that indicated he was not well. One included an incident of
vomiting and heat exhaustion. Several pilgrims saw Knight in duress
and went to tell Kevin Eubank. Eubank rushed to Knight's side and
asked him if he should go to a hospital. Knight at first refused, suggesting that to do so would be to call the power of God into question. Eubank
replied, "Then you will die here today." Knight reluctantly consented to
go, and they headed off to the hospital where Knight stayed a few days,
ultimately requesting that he be able to leave and return to the mountain
he loved. Doctors agreed, with the understanding that Eubank would
find Knight a place where he could spend time in an air-conditioned
room for most of the day. Eubank rented a small house in Niland, where

the two could live, eat healthily, rest in air-conditioning during the heat of the day, and visit the mountain regularly.

Knight's health improved, but not to the extent that the two men would have wished. After several months, it became clear that Knight needed more frequent medical care, the kind of care that could only come in a nursing care facility. It took a lot of talking and convincing to get Knight to consider leaving the mountain—he did so with the hope that one day he would return to his home and take up residence there again. One of the reasons Knight ultimately felt comfortable entering the nursing home was that he was leaving the mountain in the care of Eubank, the social worker who had lived with and cared for Knight for the past two years, and Mike Phippen, the man who had been helping around the mountain for the past several months. Knight could leave the only home he had known for thirty years because he was leaving it in the hands of people he trusted completely. Unfortunately, in December 2011, Kevin Eubank, who also struggled with heart problems and had throughout his life, died of a heart attack in his sleep. No one had seen it coming. In February 2014 Leonard Knight died. It seemed everyone had seen it coming, yet no one could believe it. He would never again return to his mountain home.

Cracks in Salvation Mountain. Photo by author.

A tire tree bearing new graffiti since Knight's death. Photo by author.

The mountain that pilgrims now explore is a disintegrating space. The desert is indeed quick to reclaim, to return the unnatural to the natural. Within months after Eubank's death, the mountain started to show serious signs of wear. The yellow-brick road was cracking; sand whipped against the paint, dulling it and enhancing the cracks opened by the sun. Those cracks may prove particularly dangerous when the rainy season comes. If water seeps into the cracks and into the adobe structure, huge segments of paint may merely slide off the mountain, as had happened to some degree on the right-hand side where "Love Is Universal" is painted. Added to that is the human wear and tear on the mountain. Visitors climb, as always, but most recently they have also started to leave their marks. Graffiti dots the mountain as more and more people attempt to mark and claim a piece of the place that seems to be anyone's and no one's. One spot declares that "Cindy was here" while another declares David's love for Celeste. Some of the most egregious occurrences of graffiti have happened on the face of the mountain—where someone signed the white outline of the heart in a dark color—and on the boat at the base of the mountain, where someone wrote in red paint on a white background, "Lamb of God have mercy on us / Lamb of God won't you grant us." For some reason, Knight's absence invites visitors to leave their own mark on the site, proving that the place no longer *feels* like someone's home. Maybe it doesn't *feel* all that sacred anymore. Instead, it may feel like a giant art installation that someone left as his mark on the world. Some visitors feel invited to share in that mark and to offer their names and use it for their own theological messages to the world.

As the mountain literally disintegrates along with the sacred space constructed through story and ritual, a vacuum has been created. No one is actively caring for the mountain in a sustained way, though some volunteers have watched over it for short periods of time, sometimes even for several months at a time. But no one has dedicated her or his life to the task. Every few months there may be a paint-party weekend, where interested people visit the mountain and work on keeping it up. Some of the mountain's caretakers have worked hard to cover the graffiti and patch the mountain's cracks. In some instances they've been able to complete tasks that Knight couldn't in his declining years, and so parts of the mountain appear in much better shape than they did when he was alive. Even so, the many hands that have contributed to the artwork are becoming apparent. The mountain shows multiple hands rather than a singular unified vision and a fully dedicated artist. Leonard Knight is not there to oversee the caretaking. He is not there to tell the stories. The mountain lacks storytellers who know Knight's stories well and want to tell them. No one is there to consistently enact its rituals.

That does not mean that visitors to the site now have an entirely different experience than those who came before Knight entered the nursing home. He did, after all, organize the space in an attempt to elicit a particular response from visitors. Visitors feel the personal aspects of the site by entering the museum, his living room. Then they may see and sense the architectural strength of the caverns to the side and recognize Knight's "famous birds" on the ceiling of those caves. Next they might climb the mountain that serves as witness to Knight's religious experience and engage the landscape—both natural and human made—in profound ways. Finally, they might descend to the base of the mountain. That is the space that has been most transformed. Where once you could sit and chat for minutes or hours with the artist under the shade of a tarp, visitors may well be alone. They will leave with their own interpretations, surely shaped by the stories that former visitors told to draw them to the mountain, but not informed so intensely by Knight's "official" set of stories and interpretations.

What happened in 2011 left a void at Salvation Mountain that was made permanent in February 2014 with Knight's death. Leonard Knight's carefully crafted space remains, but there is no official guide to help visitors move through the space. More significantly, there is no Knight there to tell the stories that mark the space as sacred. Without Knight, not only is there an eerie silence, but there is no exchange of gifts. Pilgrims may bring gifts in the form of cans of paint or money, but those gifts are not passed into other hands and the givers may not receive a thank-you. Now there is a donation box where visitors can deposit their money. No one can offer the full gift of Leonard Knight's story or offer his vision of a world where social status does not matter because all are loved by God. The mountain stands as a multivalent symbol, inviting interpretation from any passerby. Visitors do not get the "more to the story" that Knight always offered. Instead, they walk around the mountain and return to their air-conditioned cars.

Knight's ability to shape visitors' experience—the authority he drew from the space and his role in the space—is no longer there. In his absence, multiple interpretations of the space reign. This is not to say that multiple interpretations of the space didn't exist when Knight was around; it is rather to claim that Knight's understanding of the space had the aura of authority and authenticity based on his relationship to it. His interpretation operated as the official one. Now people are left to interpret and to experience for themselves.

Multiple interpretations now vie for power. People claim to have *the* authentic and authorized interpretation by claiming a close relationship to Knight. Having known and interacted with Knight operates a bit like apostolic succession in the early Christian church: "I know Knight and so I know what this space means. I am authorized to tell the story. I am authorized to paint." Or as another person who wished to remain anonymous said to me, "People are in it [preserving Salvation Mountain] for selfish reasons, thinking they are trying to do what is best but they aren't and can't because they never took the time to know Leonard." Note that this observer, who has a stake in claims to authenticity and authority, uses knowledge of Knight as a measure of whether others have the authority to interpret. But many claims to authority grow thin quickly. There is a void where Knight once stood. Will one interpretation of the space "win," and if so, which one will it be?

Leonard Knight surely understood these possibilities and wanted to maintain his control over the space even after his death. For obvious reasons, not the least of which was his thirty-year commitment to the space, Knight wanted his interpretation to remain the *official* version. Knight feared that someone with motives far different from his own would claim the space and turn it into a for-profit business. Just as much, he feared that nothing would happen, that no one would care and the mountain would simply decay. Until Kevin Eubank came along, Knight didn't know what to do about those fears. Because Eubank had worked for so long in the social service world, he was familiar with the world of nonprofits and grant applications. He began the process of setting up a board of directors for Salvation Mountain and a constitution of sorts to ensure that after Knight's death Salvation Mountain would be cared for in a way that Knight approved.

Even though Eubank did not live to see the realization of his imagined plans for the place, there is now a nonprofit board overseeing some of what happens at Salvation Mountain.[1] The board more or less has control over the site, depending on its ability to find "site supervisors" who can live at the mountain and work there. Dan Westfall, a friend of Knight's, currently serves as the board's president. The board is now called Salvation Mountain Inc. a name that points to the changes already taking place at Salvation Mountain in Knight's absence.

In 2012 the board posted a Facebook message that announced, "Salvation Mountains [*sic*] . . . first Sponsors Program." In that message, the board claimed a need for annual revenue that would go "to preserve, protect and maintain the Mountain in Leonard's absence." The board also suggested that people visit their "Amazon shopping list" and "feel free to surprise us anytime!"[2] As care for the mountain becomes necessary and Knight is no longer there to determine how things will be run, additional aspects of the capitalist exchange system have become part of the business of Salvation Mountain. The added "Inc." denotes the contradictions that have crept into the space—Salvation Mountain is no longer operating as a gift economy in the way it did when Knight was there, even while the board's goal is to preserve the charitable activity that was important to Knight.

Even so, the question of authority and authenticity has been raised more regularly since Eubank and Knight died. Many claims have been made that Knight authorized various individuals to care for the site. It is not my intention here to determine who has authority over Salvation Mountain, only to note that these vying claims have been made and continue to be made. In 2013 two rival Facebook pages existed precisely because of these vying claims to authority. In 2014, though the two pages continued to exist, there seemed to be some compromise between the different page administrators.

Sacred space is constructed and maintained through the stories that people tell about it and the rituals that they enact in it. David Chidester and Edward Linenthal have argued that sacred space is ritualized, creates meaningful worlds for its participants and, finally, is contested. They assert that "performed in a set-apart, extraordinary symbolic space, rituals can act out and embody perfectly the way things 'ought to be.'"[3] As noted, one of the rituals that can no longer be performed at Salvation Mountain is gift giving. Without the central figure of Knight present, to explain his philosophy of giving and to offer pilgrims his own gifts, without his presence to accept any gifts, the cycle of gift giving is broken. In its stead, the attempts to save Salvation Mountain, however well intentioned they may be, must rely on a capitalist system of exchange. In so doing, those attempts change people's experience of the mountain and may profoundly alter interpretations of the space.

As discussed earlier, Chidester and Linenthal claim that sacred space "is inevitably contested space, a site of negotiated contests over the legitimate ownership of sacred symbols." They elaborate, "Power is asserted and resisted in any production of space, and especially in the production of sacred space. Since no sacred space is merely 'given' in the world, its ownership will always be at stake. . . . In this respect, a sacred space is not merely discovered, or founded, or constructed; it is claimed, owned, and operated by people advancing specific interests."[4] And so, as we explore the stories of multiple interpretations of Salvation Mountain, we need to look for specific interests, for bids for power, and for attempts to claim authority and authenticity.

The example of Salvation Mountain demonstrates that sacred space is storied space and maintained space. Certainly Knight's space was contested throughout his lifetime. The State of California attempted to declare it a toxic waste site, and there are plenty of observers who would tell you that the site is a pile of junk and a waste of a person's life and time.[5] Other interpretations of the space have also been offered up by visitors to the site who value it from very different perspectives. There are as many interpretations of Salvation Mountain as there are visitors to the space. Why? Chidester and Linenthal explain that "when space or place becomes sacred, spatially scarce resources are transformed into a surplus of signification. As an arena of signs and symbols, a sacred place is not a fixed point in space, but a point of departure for an endless multiplication of mean-ing."[6] Salvation Mountain is certainly full of interpretive possibilities. Any piece of the text or image may be highlighted to support any number of interpretations. And so we are left with the question of who will gather the power to assert the next "official" interpretation of Salvation Mountain. Who has the authority? Will that interpretation look anything like Leonard Knight's? Does or should that matter?

A SIGN OF THE END TIMES AND JUDGMENT

One of the people who stepped into the void left by Knight's death was a retired man from Niland, California, who in the summer of 2012, when no one was living at or caring for the mountain, took it upon himself to sit at the mountain each day and chat with people who stopped by. Kent Walker, who has asked that his name be changed for this work, met Leonard Knight only once or twice. The first meeting occurred when his landlord asked him to take some extra paint out to the mountain for Knight to use. He remembers that Knight was overjoyed about receiving the gift.[7] Walker does not pretend that he was a friend of Knight. Rather, he feels that he is a friend of the mountain, sensing that someone should be there to greet people. He recognizes that the place is not the same without a welcoming smile, and so he has taken it upon himself to offer his presence, his own attempt to maintain the sacred space.

What stood out in my visit in the summer of 2012 is that Walker has interpreted the mountain and its message on his own, without the help of Knight and his stories, and so preaches a message to pilgrims that is different from Knight's. Walker intends to be neither inaccurate nor dis-ingenuous; he has simply interpreted the constellation of symbols on the mountain in his own way, emphasizing to visitors particular aspects of the mountain that Knight might not. It seems telling that whereas Knight's first question to visitors was most frequently "where are you from?", Walker's first question is often "have you been washed in the blood of the lamb?" This shift from *place* as a central component of iden-tity to *status* as a Christian or non-Christian indicates where Walker dif-fers from Knight.

Walker's disposition is one that lends itself to conspiracy theories. He doubts that the US government is looking after its citizens, doubts that corporations are up to anything except making Americans addicts, and doubts that there are many truly good people in the world. He spends his time listening to radio programs that challenge listeners to see all of the ways that governments and institutions are out to control them and to take away the rights they hold dear. Walker doesn't trust in much, but he does believe that Jesus died for his sins, a belief that at least on the surface gels with Knight's theology. Walker sees on one of Knight's art trucks the order to "Repent!"—a message that makes sense to him. He believes that Jesus died for the sins of the world and in blood atonement—the theology that Jesus's spilt blood was a prerequisite for humanity to have a right relationship with God. Walker preaches that we humans are debtors to God who can never repay the price that was offered in Jesus's death. Humans are simply not worthy of what they have received.

Where Knight viewed Jesus as his path toward God, offering a more open perspective on other religious traditions, Walker believes that Jesus is the only path and that even faithful believers in other traditions will, despite their faithfulness, experience eternal damnation. Walker's is a Christianity that emphasizes passages such as John 3:16 in a distinct way. Rather than interpreting the passage to be about divine love, Walker interprets it to be about Christianity's exclusive claim to the truth—that whoever does not believe in Christ as *the* savior of humanity will not receive eternal reward. Knight's interpretation was a different one: he expressed a confidence about what Jesus had done for him in his life but did not claim to know what will happen to others. Knight was concerned that people know God and God's love, not that they know it in a particular way.

For Knight, the key theological message of the mountain, his gift, is that God is love. To this Walker adds, when he describes the mountain to visitors, that God is mercy, but also that "God is . . . perfect wrath, perfect anger, perfect justice." Walker's God is one who punishes because of his love and his anger. Humans sinned and that sin is passed down through their blood. Walker claims that God then required a blood sacrifice to make things right. "If you don't believe that, you are going to perish," he says.

Walker comes to Salvation Mountain to appreciate the silence of the space, to soak up what he understands its message to be. He also believes that sometimes God calls him out to the mountain: "I come out here and occasionally I've gotten the urge from the Lord to go out to the mountain. . . . The person [who is visiting] says . . . 'I'm supposed to be here.' I don't know how he does it but God puts the words in my mouth and they hear what they need to hear. They get washed in the blood of the lamb." From Walker's perspective, "that's what Leonard made this for."[8] And so Walker believes that he is carrying on the work of Knight in Knight's stead, preaching a message about the saving power of Jesus Christ. In some ways he is like the biblical Paul, who never met Jesus but felt so confident in a shared common cause that he preached his interpretation of Jesus's message with great fervor. Walker doesn't claim authenticity by knowing Knight but claims to know exactly what Knight intended; he is confident that he and Knight both believe in the same God, the same type of Christianity. He sees evidence of a shared theology in the repentance-oriented texts on the mountain.

Cracks in the "Love Is Universal" portion of Salvation Mountain. Photo by author.

Even though he believes he is carrying on Knight's work, Walker feels comfortable critiquing that work as well. When Walker noted that the "Love Is Universal" portion of the mountain was beginning to fall down, he felt it was evidence that God did not like what it said and argued that that was the portion of Knight's mountain "where he went wrong." That's "new age," he asserted, "not Christian." He argued that God may love all, but that did not mean that God's love was universal. God hates evil and sin. God will punish those who do not accept Jesus as their lord and savior. Walker interprets the mountain within his own theological framework, and that interpretation includes pointing out where he thinks Knight went wrong.

Even so, Walker agrees with most of what he believes the mountain is communicating. Being a premillennial dispensationalist, he explains that we are in the final era, or "dispensation," before the Second Coming of Christ. That event will be preceded by a period of trials and tribulations in the world when it will appear that evil is going to win out. As a believer in this type of Christianity, Walker holds that the Second Coming of Christ is imminent, though he thinks it will go down in a way quite different from what Knight has envisioned. Walker asserts that the Imperial Valley has an identical geography to the Middle East. For visitors he draws a map of the Imperial Valley in which the Salton Sea lines up over the Dead Sea and each geographical phenomenon in Israel has its counterpart in California. This geography lesson indicates to Walker that the Imperial Valley will play a central role in the Second Coming. Even more central to Walker is Salvation Mountain, whose future indicates who is winning in the battle between good and evil. Walker argues that the "window is closing. . . . If [Salvation Mountain] were to be 'destroyed,' from the rain . . . God's rain . . . the window is closed. When this place is gone, the game is over." Salvation Mountain's disintegration indicates the rule of evil, "or, this place is going to be saved, repainted. And when God's wrath comes upon the nation and the world, this place will be a rallying place for his people." Walker explains, "Which way it goes, I don't have a clue, it could go either way."[9] He reads the mountain as central to the map of the future coming of Christ. Slab City and its surrounding areas, including Niland, where there is so much poverty and drug use, are evidence that the space surrounding the sacred place is evil. According to Walker, God called Knight to that place in order to be a voice for good in the world, a voice crying out in the wilderness. His message is God's message, one that will hopefully win out.

Walker does his own work in an attempt to mark the space as sacred, even while acknowledging that the space is not his. His stories become the interpretive framework for many a visitor because Knight is not there to offer his own interpretation. Walker's message is certainly a form of Christian theology, and Knight might have found much on which he and Walker agreed.

Some of Walker's theological arguments may sound farfetched—his beliefs about the Second Coming and the centrality of Salvation Mountain as well as his ideas about the government's conspiracy to enslave its citizens are certainly not mainstream arguments. Yet Walker's interpretation of Salvation Mountain is perhaps better understood as an extreme version of the interpretations of many evangelicals who come to the site. Walker sees the Second Coming as radiating outward from Salvation Mountain—the status of the mountain being a sign of how the battle between good and evil in the world is going.

When he looks at the mountain, Walker focuses his eyes on the heart with the sinner's prayer. That heart, coupled with the Lord's Prayer and "Repent" on the roof of one of Knight's trucks, tap into several traditional Christian theological symbol systems. Thus, many evangelicals, including Walker, can see the mountain as evidence of the truthfulness of his belief system while at the same time pinpointing aspects of the mountain's text as "wrong." "Love Is Universal" does not jive with Walker's world view, and he believes that "God Is love" should be followed by "and wrath, and judgment," yet he claims the mountain is truth. Here we see an example of how community shapes how and what we see in profound ways. When Walker sees something that does not fit into his interpretive framework—something that doesn't fit within the Christian symbolic system he has been taught—he does not adjust the framework to overcome the cognitive dissonance. Rather, he uses the framework to explain what he sees: God is causing the paint that reads "Love Is Universal" to come off the mountain. In making this claim, Walker creates resonance between what he sees and what he believes he knows to be true.

It is important to note that there is a profound difference between Knight's and Walker's theology. Walker's is not a form of prophetic speech. It is the type of message that people could hear in Christian churches throughout the United States. It is not, as one scholar of prophecy notes about the words of prophets, an "insight unavailable to the majority of the audience."[10] It is not speech that calls the community to change its ways or speech that imagines a different future. Rather, it is an accepting speech, a speech that accepts that the world is not as it ought to be and imagines a future full of God's anger and punishment for human failures. It imagines a better life cannot be had in this world. Walker's message, at least the theology of blood atonement and the exclusivity of Christian claims, can be found in many churches. It can be found in the Christian rock music of the band Third Day, which will be discussed below. It can be heard in the sermons of televangelists every Sunday morning. It is not the speech of an outsider; it is thoroughly mainstream. Leonard Knight's speech was different. Knight's was the message that pilgrims sought out, the one they traveled thousands of miles to hear. They came to see his medium, but they also came to *feel* his message. And that seems to be distinctly tied to the prophetic nature of his speech that imagined a world as it ought to be.

EVANGELICAL WITNESS AND INSPIRATION

Picture this: the Christian rock band Third Day—a band that sounds like the offspring of a marriage between Dave Matthews and Hootie and the Blowfish and has repeatedly hit it big on both Christian and secular music charts—sings its album's title song, "Revelation," while fans wave their hands in the air in response to the band's Christian witness. Behind the four band members, Mac Powell (singer), Tai Anderson (bassist), Mark Lee (guitarist), and David Carr (drums), is a Jumbotron that displays video footage of a tour of Salvation Mountain.[11] In fact, *Salvation Mountain* was the working title of the album. The mountain itself served as an inspiration for band members, and creator Leonard Knight's

dedication to expressing his faith through his art makes him a model
Christian in their eyes. And it is for this reason that Salvation Mountain
appears on the Jumbotron, as skinny jeans–clad, long-haired, bearded
Mac Powell sings, "My life has led me down the road that's so uncertain /
And now I am left alone and I am broken, / Tryin' to find my way, tryin'
to find the faith that's gone." Though "Revelation" begins in uncertainty
and doubt, the singer calls on God: "Give me a revelation, / Show me
what to do / 'Cause I've been tryin' to find my way, / I haven't got a clue."
The only surety comes with the knowledge that Powell has "got nothing"
without God. As bassist Tai Anderson has expressed, the song has more
questions than answers: "God puts a light to our feet, not a floodlight to
our future. I think God wants us coming back to Him for help."[12] Though
the members of Third Day feel comfortable expressing a certain amount
of doubt in their lyrics, they nonetheless see in Knight a fellow evangelist
who uses the medium of his artwork to call out to Christians to rededi-
cate their lives to Christ and to find the only possibility of salvation in a
Christian path.

So how is it that Third Day came to view Knight's mountain as a point
of inspiration and to see Salvation Mountain as a symbol of the band's
message? What led them to believe they shared theological and social
ground with Leonard Knight? Part of the explanation comes in the common experience of being "born again," an experience many evangelical
Christians claim. An evangelical world view and an understanding of
born-again experiences as the central experience in a Christian life shapes
the way evangelicals *see* Salvation Mountain. More accurately, it shapes
what they see and *what they do not see* there. That world view has led thousands of evangelical Christians, including members of Third Day, to see
Knight as a kindred Christian spirit and an authentic Christian voice.

The Christian rock movement of which Third Day is a part stands in
a long tradition within the history of Christianity of using popular
media—barroom songs, radio, and commercial jingles, for example—to
communicate the Christian message to an ever-changing audience.
Because it is the music of Saturday night merged with Sunday morning,
Christian rock has the ability to transcend traditional denominational
boundaries and divisions. At the same time the music has been an

effective tool of communicating the Christian message to sometimes disenfranchised populations; in many congregations it has become the music of Sunday morning as churches try to claim it as part of their own communal traditions. We might even go so far as to say that Christian rock has become *the music of the everyday* for its fans. In so doing, it shapes the daily identity of its listeners and may well play a larger role in their identity formation than the "hallowed rites and dramatic events" of their religious institutions.[13] As historian of religious radio Tona Hangen reminds us, "What believers do over and over again not only reinforces their perceptions of reality but comes to constitute their reality as well."[14]

The message of the music, most often of conservative cultural values and of conservative evangelical theology, becomes the shared cultural norms of fans. The fans have created a subculture, one they believe is set over and against mainstream culture. Fans of Christian rock music believe they are in this world but not of this world. They are—from their perspective—a people set apart.

This may be true. Christian rock not only spans denominational divisions but also brings together people from different segments of society. However, the adherents of the Christian evangelical culture are largely "white, primarily conservative and rural (in spirit if not residence), Protestant [Christians who] account for 23 percent of all Americans."[15] Christian rock, then, also represents the evangelical acceptance of the media industry and its attempts to use that media for its own purposes. Christian rock CDs, T-shirts, and other items "help forge a place for contemporary, middle-class, white evangelicals in modern American consumer culture." They help this demographic claim a stake as "a viable demographic of savvy, up-to-date consumers."[16] In purchasing Christian rock music, fans declare that they are individuals with "*respectability* in a country in which people are most often addressed by mass culture not as citizens but as consumers."[17] While their wallets allow them to claim a stake as "average Americans," their sense of self and of their identity as persecuted Christians continues to bind them to one another.

That this group is able to *feel* like an outcast minority while not actually being one numerically is tied to its culture as well as its theological values. Oppression and persecution are celebrated within this segment of Christianity as aspects of being Christlike. Feeling persecuted binds together the members of the subculture and reinforces a sense of identity. Outsiders who claim that Christian rock is simply *bad* rock 'n' roll, then, end up fitting into evangelicals' narrative about themselves as a persecuted, misunderstood people. As one historian of Christian rock has suggested, this genre has "an arguably deserved reputation as the least fashionable music on earth."[18]

And it is in the midst of these narratives that members of the band Third Day literally grew up. Claiming that they were influenced musically by such bands as Lynyrd Skynyrd, U2, and Rich Mullins, multiplatinum Third Day was equally influenced by its Christian identity. The band has openly tried to reconcile its Christian and rock 'n' roll identities for the public. The group debuted in 1996 with a self-titled work. By 2000 two more albums, *Time* and *Offerings,* appeared. The latter was followed in 2003 with its twin, *Offerings II.* The next year the band's album *Wire* appeared, followed by its release of *Revelation* in 2008. In that same year, Third Day won the American Music Award. And the awards have piled up: "The band has earned 27 No. 1 singles and sold more than 7 million albums which reflect 2 RIAA Platinum and 9 Gold Certifications. A recent Georgia Music Hall of Fame inductee (2009), Third Day has garnered 24 career GMA Dove Awards from 42 nominations, 4 GRAMMY Awards (with 11 career nominations), an American Music Award . . . , 3 American Music Award nominations and multiple ASCAP honors for songwriting."[19] Perhaps most indicative of the band's success in the secular world was its appearance on the *Tonight Show with Jay Leno* in order to launch *Revelation.*

Though the group has achieved much success, it has experienced some negative backlash because of its decidedly Christian identity. "Two high-profile publications actually pulled their reviews of a Third Day album after [Third Day's publicist] sent reviewers the CD booklet, which mentioned the Bible," notes historian of Christian rock Heather Hendershot.[20] Unlike U2's Bono, Third Day's band members have taken up the expected traits of the fans they represent. Accepting the award for Special Event Album of the Year, one band member thanked God for enabling the group to appear on an album tied to the popular film *The Passion of the Christ* because it allowed them "the opportunity to perform on the [*Tonight Show*]." When they won the Rock/Contemporary Album of the Year award, Mac Powell asked the audience to join him in a prayer: "If there's anything in the industry that's not of you [God] . . . we pray you take it out."[21] As a Christian rock hero, Powell declared his identity as not-of-this-world to a crowd filled with both believers and nonbelievers. In so doing, he stood out as a representative of the subculture of evangelical Christians.

Like Leonard Knight, the members of Third Day claim that the medium and the message must coincide in some way. Seeing Knight as their own heroic figure, one who has eschewed the trappings of this world, Third Day has been inspired by his work. They encountered Knight's mountain almost by accident when they did a video close to the Salton Sea. In preparation, they watched a documentary about the area that discussed Salvation Mountain. The band then "drew inspiration from Salvation Mountain to create the album art" in order to send their own message of "God's love to the world."[22] The band's guitarist, Tai Anderson, recalls that the band saw something special in Salvation Mountain, a shared artistic vision: "There was just something crazy and beautiful about taking trash and making something beautiful out of it. There's something kind of frightening, but attractive about a man who would commit his life to constructing something like that. I think a lot of people hear the message of our music, and feel the same way."[23]

Feeling a kindred spirit with Knight as Christian artists, the band initially planned to use Salvation Mountain as its inspirational art form and as a title for the album: "'Wouldn't it be great if we came up with something cool like Salvation Mountain?' We wanted to make this art attractive and interesting. When you look at [Salvation Mountain], you wonder is this person crazy? He's built a monument to God in the middle of the desert. Every day he adds more to it. It's . . . eclectic . . . strange . . . different . . . so dramatic."[24] The band saw Knight's Salvation Mountain as inspiration not only because of its final product but also because the mountain reflects a faith journey, one they believe they share with Knight. Tai Anderson suggests that "it's a good metaphor for us as a Christian band. People say, 'That's strange. Why are you a Christian band? How does [your] faith compel [you] to do this thing?' It seemed like a cool metaphor for where we are right now. . . . It's an evolving thing, so we'll see how it shapes up."[25]

And so Salvation Mountain served as symbol for band members of commitment to art and to faith. Although the inspiration of Salvation Mountain was not ultimately represented in the album's title (after the band recorded the song "Revelation" it decided that that was the right title), Salvation Mountain was represented on its cover, in a graphic designer's "folk version" of the mountain. Actual photographs of the mountain appear in the CD's inner materials. Some critics believe that the folk cover was actually a copycat version of Radiohead's *Hail to the Thief* CD cover. Defenders of the band's reputation were equally adamant. "If you actually buy the CD, you'd open it up to find lots of actual photographs of Salvation Mountain, and see that the cover art looks pretty much just like it," wrote one fan. "It's such an inspirational place, I think it's perfect for Third Day to use it for their art . . . to help people find SALVATION! Salvation Mountain/Salvation . . . see the theme here?"[26]

Not surprisingly, the band also defended its graphic designer and its choice of Salvation Mountain as an inspiration. Tai Anderson described how Mac Powell had been inspired by Salvation Mountain and that they were surprised as soon as they heard the understandable criticisms: "As soon as the cover imagery was released, we started reading critiques that we had ripped off Radiohead's *Hail to the Thief.* When you lay them side by side, there are obvious similarities. But we weren't referencing outside sources when we were tweaking the designs and ideas that our label designer was coming up with."[27]

Though the accusations of copycat behavior of both their medium and their CD covers continue, Third Day still works to communicate a particular theology to its fans. That theology binds them together as a community with a shared set of values—one that sees its center as salvation, one they believe they share with Leonard Knight.

Third Day articulates their theology in their lyrics. Like Knight, the songwriters and band members argue that their culture has become problematic in many different ways. Third Day's 2008 album *Revelation* is testament to such claims. Its songs describe individuals who do not feel loved, who do not believe they have a place in the world, and who see the world as too materialistic. The world is moving too quickly, Third Day says in its song "Slow Down." It is a rat race: "Tell me to slow down if you see / That I'm runnin' too fast in the wrong race. / Tell me to slow down if you think / That I can't keep up with my own pace." The song begs someone who knows better to slow down the runner. "Oh, I don't want to let go," croons the singer, "of all the things that I know / Are keepin' me away from my life."[28] On the album itself, the sense that the singer is going nowhere fast and needs guidance from somewhere else is coupled with a critique of the narcissism that runs rampant in American culture.

The antidote to consumerism and narcissism is found in an obscure reference to a God who loves without cease. The consistent message throughout the album is that God has a constant love that never fails, one appreciated and valued as a guidepost in life's journeys. In fact, in the refrain of the song titled "Revelation," the singer claims that he has "got nothing without You." Standing in a long Christian tradition of merging the metaphor of human love with a passionate, loving relationship with the divine, Third Day offers its listeners the possibility of a very intimate connection with a God who loves unconditionally.

At the same time, the band seems to embrace the modern theology of the prosperity gospel, a theology that suggests that a positive faith and active Christian attitude and ministry will bring material wealth to believers. Perhaps nowhere is this clearer than in band pastor Nigel James's *Lessons from the Road*. In it James writes, "We all need to develop our full potential—God can make our lives both prosperous and meaningful—but we always must remember God's part, depend on Him and offer Him due credit and thanksgiving." James argues that God is in control and implies that wealth and prosperity are indications of divine favor in human activity. If God controls everything, an individual's life becomes evidence of that individual's relationship with God. According to James, those who find success in the Christian music industry must remember who they are and remain humble, knowing that God brought them their wealth and popularity.[29]

That path to a mutual relationship with God begins with being born again, a common experience shared among evangelical Christians, who describe it as a literal rebirth that comes with a realization of sinful nature and a rededication to living in relationship with Jesus. This rebirth is accompanied by a commitment to attempt to live without actively sinning against God. In Third Day's song "Born Again," the singer claims that he was lost when "you found me here, / And I was broken beyond repair, / Then You came along and sang Your song over me." The band croons that redemption lies only in surrender to the truth of blood atonement, that Jesus shed his blood in order to redeem humanity from its sinful nature and to allow humans the possibility of achieving eternal heavenly reward. For fans, the appeal of Third Day's theology rests in its promise that with God, an individual can "live forever."

Perhaps nowhere is the difference between Knight's and Third Day's response to the trappings of this world clearer than in Third Day's documentary-style film *Live Revelations*. It is here that the band members identify with not just the theology of conservative evangelicals but also with their social world view. They identify family as a relation between a heterosexual, monogamous couple, one that has created offspring as the mainstay of its existence. A scene that depicts Mac Powell's father coming to a concert and declaring himself one of the band's "best fans" is followed fairly quickly by the band members attending the soccer games of their kids and taking playground trips to the park with their children so that their wives can have a break. They sentimentalize the family and the events of family life they have to miss to be part of the band: "I missed my son's football season, I missed the school play . . . all of those little things that people mark their lives by."[30]

If their lifestyles are so different from Knight's, what allows Third Day band members and other evangelicals to claim him as a kindred spirit? What is it that shapes what evangelicals see and don't see at Salvation Mountain? They often arrive knowing the story of Leonard Knight—that his born-again experience led him to live in the desert for decades, building a mountain for God. With that bit of knowledge, they feel they know that he is kin. The sense of kinship is reinforced by the name of the space—Salvation Mountain. For the evangelical Christians I met, the name profoundly shaped their expectations. They felt they were coming to see the place where a man built a mountain because of his confidence that the death of Jesus secured his own salvation.

What they see, then, is confirmation of these expectations. Our expectations are shaped by the stories we hear, by the world views we hold, and by the cultures in which we live. Those expectations mold our vision. Evangelical visitors focus their gaze on the giant cross that crowns the mountain and their eyes drop to see the sinner's prayer emblazoned in the heart on the face of the mountain. It is through their understanding that Jesus died for their sins that they interpret the space in between. The God that they often imagine is a disciplinarian father who doles out punishment and reward based on the child's behavior, a God whose main task is to hold people accountable. "God is love" does not mean that God does not judge and punish those who do not have a born-again experience and do not accept Jesus Christ as their Lord and Savior. It is through the lens of their understanding of being born again that they read the text of the mountain.

The persecuted-minority narrative—that evangelicals are a marginalized group in American society—gets applied to Leonard Knight and his project. One retiree visiting Salvation Mountain reflected a narrative I heard several times during my time there: he told me that he was so sad that Knight had to go all the way into the middle-of-nowhere desert in order to build his mountain because no one would have let him build it any closer to a populated area. In this instance, the oppressed-minority narrative was read onto Knight's story. The visitor suggested that the larger culture was so secular, in fact, *anti*-Christian, that no one would have tolerated such a flagrant display of love for Jesus anywhere near "civilization." From this perspective, Knight became a hero, a man willing to stand against a culture that hates him precisely because he declares his love for God. Knight's journey was explained as a flight from a culture that could not tolerate a true Christian to the desert where he could freely express his faith. Such visitors imagine Knight as an outsider, standing apart from the secular world in which he lived. They ground their claims to kinship with Knight in the idea that they too are persecuted in American culture for the Christian faith that defines their identity.

Evangelical visitors to the mountain also appreciate Knight's critique of the materialism of this world. They are moved by his sense of freedom and see its roots in the Christian message. Though they will return to their own social locations and participation in a capitalist system, they admire Knight for living that aspect of their faith.

Many evangelical visitors to the mountain also connect with Knight's commitment. They see their own dedication to their faith reflected in his thirty-year commitment to his mountain. They recognize his singularity of vision and identify it with their own. They interpret Knight's work and his critique of this world as speaking to the promise of a future. While Knight would surely not argue with those interpretations, these visitors' vision of the future is often quite different from Knight's. Knight was a postmillennialist and viewed the future as moving toward more and more love. Premillennialists read his mountain as symbolic of a future that will be filled with trials and tribulations in this world followed by a triumph of good over evil. Those different visions of the future rarely came up in discussions between Knight and his visitors. There is enough symbolic evidence in the mountain for evangelicals that they assume a shared vision. The cross, the sinner's prayer, the biblical verses covering the mountain, the name of the mountain itself—all symbolically endorse their interpretation of the mountain. They *know* it is evidence of the truthfulness of the experience they share with Knight.

The sinner's prayer on the face of Salvation Mountain. Photo by author.

These evangelical interpretations were offered several times by speakers at Knight's memorial service at Salvation Mountain. Those who read the mountain this way focused on the text inside the heart. As one of Knight's eulogists, Patrick Rea, described it, "Leonard had his job and God has his job and it's all right there on that heart. It's a matter of the heart." Here Rea describes the heart on the mountain as its central text and expresses a sense that the mountain's effect on visitors is a change in their own hearts, a renewal of spiritual understanding. One of Knight's nephews also focused on the heart in his eulogy, seeing it as a symbol of how Knight brought him to Christianity and as a sign of their born-again status: "It's great to see 'Say Jesus I'm a sinner. Please come upon my body and into my heart.' That's how my uncle led me to the Lord."

It may well be that this is the interpretation of Salvation Mountain that will win out in the end. Since Knight left the mountain, more language about the importance of repentance has appeared there. Perhaps the most obvious, if for no other reason than its size, is that a second roof of a structure built on the back of a truck has been placed alongside the first, both painted white with four-foot red letters instructing the viewer to "Repent!" Now when a visitor stands at the top of Salvation Mountain and surveys the view down below, that visitor sees two roofs proclaiming repentance as the key to salvation. The mountain thus serves as symbol of what is taught in evangelical sermons every Sunday morning—that the heart is the key to faith, that salvation is offered through Jesus's blood, and that to join the church is to stand against the culture as a persecuted minority.

TOXIC TRASH HEAP OR TRASHY TRESPASS?

In 1994 Salvation Mountain's sacred status was threatened, and the threat came in the guise of environmental testers who determined that the soil at the site had been contaminated by the thousands of gallons of paint that Knight had poured onto his mountain (see chapter 6). To Knight and his supporters, it appeared that the state was claiming that the sacred was, in fact, profane. Those were fighting words.

Knight and his friends hired their own testers in order to challenge the state's interpretation of the mountain. They saw a sacred piece of artwork. The state saw a toxic trash heap standing in the way of its desire to turn Slab City into a pay campsite. In the end, Knight's supporters were able to "prove" that the soil was not contaminated, and from their perspective, that reaffirmed the site's sacred status. The story they told was about their interpretation of the space winning the day.

Now that Knight is gone, several of the questions that arose in 1994 are starting to bubble to the surface again. No one has yet claimed that the site is toxic, but people are starting to wonder what will happen to the land that Knight trespassed on for decades. Now that he is gone, won't someone step in to claim it? Will the people who are trying to save Salvation Mountain also be tolerated trespassers on someone else's land?

The land on which Salvation Mountain sits was first given to the State of California by the federal government when it became a state in 1850. Before the 1848 Treaty of Guadalupe Hidalgo, which ended the United States' war with Mexico, that same land was part of Mexico. The US government used the land during World War II as a military base. It was then that the government put in the slabs that remain as the foundation of Slab City. The land reverted back to the state in the 1960s. Nonetheless, the exact boundaries of the state's property are not entirely clear. California State Lands Commission's chief officer, Curtis Fossum, is confident that the state owns the land adjacent to Slab City but isn't entirely certain about Salvation Mountain. According to one news source, "The state hasn't had the resources it would take to find out. As Fossum points out, 'the Land Commission manages over four and a half million acres, and Salvation Mountain sits on less than one of those acres. We are a small office. We don't have the ability to go down there and fence it off. We don't have the funding for it. But we'll be looking at those issues in the coming year.'"[31] If the state shows continued interest in the site and has a vision of how the land might be used differently, Salvation Mountain may not survive in the coming years. In such a fragile environment as the desert, concerns about the quality of land and water are of the utmost importance. If it is proven that Salvation Mountain does affect these environmental resources, the case against it will be strong.

Since Knight's death, concern about who owns the land and its surrounds continues to come up. Salvation Mountain Inc. has begun discussions with the state over purchasing the land it is on. At the same time, fans of Container Charlie's artwork are pursuing the purchase of his home and art garden. There are even residents of Slab City who are organizing and attempting to raise funds to buy the land there in order to protect its way of life. Some residents feel it is the only way to preserve the last "free" place in America. Others argue that with the simple act of purchase, the place itself will lose its freedom. That purchase represents a bid for power, they argue, and will ultimately bring about class differences and institutional affiliations. It will bring *government*.[32]

In the question of whether the state will claim Salvation Mountain, the government does not need to claim authenticity, because it claims authority drawn from a different source. Whereas Knight's authority rested in religious experience and prophetic speech, implying that the ultimate authority for his activities lay with God, the state claims authority as a governmental institution. Just as the Roman government did not need to challenge Jesus's claims to speak for God, neither does the State of California need to challenge Knight's authority. The Roman government merely had to assert that Jesus was *breaking the law* in order to challenge the authority Jesus had with the people. The State of California need only declare the site toxic or its caretakers squatters to affirm its claims about the space.

The status of Salvation Mountain is not secure. In part that instability is tied to its history—Knight never asked who owned that land before he set up shop there. Future caretakers will also be squatters; they have no other choice. Yet the philosophy of the place is changing. The new board of directors demonstrates a shift in the place. As institutions are created and money is collected in a systematic way, the place automatically becomes different from the space that Knight set up with his pilgrims. These institutional structures, however basic they may be, run counter to the squatter philosophy of Knight's freedom in the desert. Institutions breed more institutions, and more and more people are stepping in to help, creating documents and structures in an attempt to maintain what was created outside of documents, structures, and capitalist exchange. Can these institutions uphold the site's sacred status as their mode of maintaining the space changes? Will visitors continue to find the space worth visiting? Will people continue to give gifts—things like paint and money—when their gift has been commodified and measured in new ways? If they do, will it *feel* the same?

JUST PLAIN WEIRD

It could well be that Knight's Salvation Mountain will go down in the history books as the incredibly odd creation of an extremely odd man. No one could claim that Knight's life path was ordinary. In fact, some have declared that he is just plain crazy, a social dropout who couldn't think of anything better to do with his life. What prompted him to move to the middle of nowhere to build not one but two mountains? The individuals who interpret Salvation Mountain in this way tend to fall into two camps: those who appreciate the unique artistry of the place and those who think it is *just plain weird*. Though I am grouping these individuals together, they are quite distinct from previous interpretations. Whereas some interpretations are exclusivist—no other interpretation could be equally true and valid at the same time—the "weird" and the "unique artistry" camp (as well as the interpretation discussed in the next section) can be viewed as inclusivist. They can operate alongside other interpretations and possibly overlap with other interpretations. For example, one could claim that Knight and his project are weird while also accepting the religious and social claims that he makes, allowing that the oddness of the medium (the mountain) or the strangeness of the artist does not negate the truthfulness of the message.

What do these assertions that Salvation Mountain is weird look like? As discussed in chapter 6, a tourism book titled *Weird California* (part of a series of books that explore the odd, strange, and weird in all of the fifty states of the United States) includes Knight. Knight's work can be found amid such intriguing artifacts as "Tess, the Fifty-Foot-Tall Woman," the "World's Largest Rubber Band Ball," the "Cranky Old Man's Cement Garden," and "Grandma Prisbrey's Bottle Village."[33] Here, Salvation Mountain appears as the type of oddity described in Timothy Beal's *Roadside Religion*. Beal notes that work like Knight's is outrageous because it is so self-revelatory—any passerby can be a witness to the innermost workings, the home life, and the belief system of the artist: "It is above all this outrageous gesture of self-exposure, this desire to communicate a very personal, perhaps incommunicable religious experience in such a public, even spectacular way that . . . [is] so personally disarming. It's an invitation to relationship, with . . . anyone who visits."[34] That Knight was open to relationship with anyone made him unique in American culture. That his private world was open *always* for public scrutiny, that his life was on display, made him an oddity.

What attracts people to such works as Knight's is the way the artwork transgresses boundaries. It is natural and supernatural, sacred and profane, otherworldly and thisworldly. Knight dared to use the desert—its broken-down cars, dried-up clay, and leftover paint—to create a piece of artwork that expresses his most profound religious experience. That oddity, as well as the skill that Knight developed to create the oddity, draws people to Salvation Mountain. These individuals may well not have different experiences today than they would when Knight was present. They have come to witness the odd and strange of human experience and creativity, not to meet a so-called prophet. Their interpretive lens is shaped by the culture in which they live. That culture tells them that home and religion are private matters. It is therefore automatic to view the spectacle of Knight's boundary transgressions as strange and weird. Their culture tells them this is true, and by applying terms like "strange" and "weird" to Knight, they reaffirm their status as "normal," as proper viewers according to cultural norms.

What of the folks in the other camp who go to see Knight precisely because his mountain is out-of-the-way outsider art? What can explain their pilgrimages to the site? What do they experience at the mountain? What of those who see Knight's mountain as unique artistry?

They came and they continue to come because they enjoy American folk art or religious art. Some pilgrims see Knight as an artist and his mountain as art, first and only. One such visitor claimed that the mountain "really evokes a sense of fantasy that so many adults seem to lose." He suggested that the "ideas expressed in the work may not be Mr. Knight's creations [because they were rooted in the biblical text], but his media and forms of expression are impressive partly because they are distinctly *of* Mr. Knight."[35] Often artists themselves, these visitors do not see bad art or bad religion, they see art that they view as legitimate and unique: "My own artistic process is much like Knight's. . . . I begin with my experiences and work from there. That is what makes my art *my art*."[36] That they recognize artistry does not mean they do not see Knight as an individual who has made some strange choices. "It was amazing to see a kind of art I've never seen before. In the middle of nowhere to build this mountain . . . [is] unbelievably crazy," noted one visitor.[37] The "craziness" attributed to Knight is recognized by some; for others it is *the* primary motivation for heading out to the desert. These visitors also see Knight and his mountain as outsiders, outsiders to the art world and its stranglehold on understandings of taste. In treasuring Knight's art, they intentionally place themselves, too, outside of what mainstream culture deems normal.

SECULARIZED POSTMILLENNIALISM

Third Day is not the only musical group to be inspired by Leonard Knight and his message. And the differences between Third Day and Coldwater Jane are vast: one is a rock band, the other a country-pop combo; one worships a resurrected Jesus who died on the cross in its lyrics, the other steers clear of promoting any particular religious message. And yet Salvation Mountain still serves as a meaningful symbol and inspiration for both sets of artists. Coldwater Jane interprets the mountain as a vision of the future when love spreads around the globe. Theirs is an inclusive interpretation and one that is representative of an interpretation of Salvation Mountain embraced by many younger visitors. These visitors are drawn to the message of a universal love of all people and even appreciate that Knight's message is *for him* rooted in a Christian theology. However, they reject the source of Knight's message while claiming the content for themselves. These visitors see love as the core message of the mountain and tend to ignore those aspects of it that seem "too religious," such as the "Repent!" emblazoned in red on art trucks at the base of the mountain.

The video for Coldwater Jane's first hit song, "Bring On the Love," begins with a young girl watching television. As she stares at the glowing screen, a newscaster's voice announces that there is "breaking news in the case of that horrific abuse story out of West Virginia." The camera quickly leaves the young girl watching television and moves to the two blonde sisters, Brandon Jane and Leah Crutchfield, who make up Coldwater Jane, a country-pop duo that sounds like the Dixie Chicks meets 1980s pop. The rest of the video follows the two women and many children as they dance around Salvation Mountain and the broken-down automobiles surrounding it. Even Leonard Knight makes several appearances, holding up his two thumbs and swaying to the beat, teaching children something (we cannot hear what), and smiling. While dancing and swinging their arms as an expression of joy and freedom, the duo sings, "I drink my coke / I read the paper / I sit and listen to the 6 o'clock news / It's like the whole world's / gone to pieces / And we're all part of the wrecking crew." Beginning on a note that sounds rather hopeless, the song then declares that there "ain't nothing so broke / We can't fix it." And what is the "fix it" solution? "Bring on the love / I know you got it in ya / Bring on the Love . . . / Ain't nothing else that's gonna make it right / So bring on the love." The duo's website declares that the song is a "guitar driven plea for peace and understanding both in personal relationships and in the world at large."[38] In an interview, Leah Crutchfield described writing the song, noting that "the melody and title came out pretty quickly since we were just having fun. The next day we came in and wrote what we wanted to say. Kind of a 'come together,' love everybody kind of tune. It was important for us to say something that had meaning, but still be able to write it in an encouraging light."[39] It is here that the pair sees a kindred spirit in Leonard Knight. He too wanted and envisioned a future when love and peace will reign in the world. Though the duo makes no religious claims in the song, they nonetheless view Knight's mountain as a symbol expressing the future that they imagine for everyone, one of peaceful coexistence.

Brandon and Leah both grew up in the town of Lucedale, Mississippi, with a population of less than three thousand. Their father was a "'70s rocker at heart" and encouraged his daughters to participate in music when the family went on tour as a family gospel band. The family ties run deep for Coldwater Jane; in fact, their name is a combination of the name of a famous canyon in Los Angeles, Coldwater Canyon, and a female name that runs in the family, Jane. The sisters believe that the name reminds them "of the '70s bands they both loved such as the Eagles, Tom Petty and the Heartbreakers and Fleetwood Mac." Their inspirations include those bands along with Emmylou Harris, Patty Griffin, Linda Ronstadt, and Patty Loveless.[40]

Coldwater Jane's song describes a postmillennial vision of a peaceful and loving future, one much different than the world today. Even though the song embraces Knight's postmillennialism, Coldwater Jane secularizes the message. This secularized postmillennialism does not pinpoint God as the moving agent in the peaceful future but simply asks its listeners to "bring on the love." Salvation Mountain serves as a flexible symbol and inspiration for those who want to critique the present world and hope for a radically different future. The two singers have literally stood on its prophetic platform and suggested through song that the world could be different. Though they do not claim, through their music or any other aspect of their persona, the critiques that Knight has made of his culture, they claim his vision of the future. In hoping for a future filled with love, Coldwater Jane embraces Knight's prophetic vision and secularizes it. Love, they say, is all we need. The duo makes no mention of God; in fact, the agent in the song is the audience—the audience should bring down the love as an antidote to all that is wrong in the world. The future will be better, the song promises, with an Eden-like future that anyone can help bring into being.

Coldwater Jane's lyrics portray a broken world in need of fixing for the sake of the children. The world has gone to pieces but has a simple solution: "Ain't no big mystery / Ain't rocket science / Don't take a genius to figure it out." All that the world needs is "a little mercy / A little kindness / Yeah baby ain't that what it's all about." The duo claims Knight's vision of the future and love as the antidote to the world's ailments. They do not critique what Knight pinpoints as the causes of people feeling unloved, the rat-race economy and the boundaries set between themselves and others in order to create and maintain social hierarchies. In removing the religious world view from the message, they also remove the critique of social structures that Knight embedded in his world view. Where evangelical Kent Walker and Third Day see "Repent!" and the sinner's prayer as the primary texts of the Mountain, Coldwater Jane sees "Love" and, in it, a hope for the future. For them, Knight's mountain serves as a symbol of potential: the world could indeed move toward more radical love, and the site of its origin could well be found in the middle-of-nowhere desert.

Coldwater Jane's is not the only interpretation of the mountain that stands in this line of secularized postmillennialism. Another musical version of this vision came out on YouTube immediately following Leonard Knight's death. Kylie Campion, a visitor to the mountain, posted a video of herself singing "Salvation Mountain (Slab City)." A recording of the song was also played at Knight's memorial service at Salvation Mountain. In the song Campion explains,

Way out east of the Salton Sea
The desert took a hold of me
And has since never let me go
I've got a hand drawn map to get from place to place
Lines of mud across my face
No way to understand unless you know
Unless you know . . .

The first stanza of Campion's song indicates that there are secrets to be found in the desert, particularly at Salvation Mountain. Secrets that people cannot know unless they go there. That feeling or knowledge that she found in the desert has captured Campion and changed her understanding of self and the world.

Campion continues: "Rivers flow / Freedom rings / The wise old white-haired man who sings / Told me once what it means to love."[41] Here Campion points out what, for her, is the central message of both Knight and Salvation Mountain: Love. Another stanza of the song provides a note of hope for the future: "Doors of cars / Bales of hay / Words of truth on paint and clay / May not change the world but it's a start." The song embraces a message about spreading love into the future, hoping for a change. Again God is not the active agent of the love, but the love is key. Perhaps this secularized post-millennial interpretation is best summed up in a Facebook post written in February 2014, not long after Knight died: "Love is love, is love. Thank you for your message to the world."[42] Here the poster sees love when looking at the mountain. Though that love does not appear to be particularly active, it is still interpreted as a much needed and often missing message to the world. Viewers in this camp interpret "love" or, in the words of Rebecca Hoffberger, "love based participation" as the sole message of the mountain.

A DECAYING DREAM

Perhaps it is the desert that will claim the final interpretation of Salvation Mountain. Perhaps the desert winds, its ferocious if brief rains, and its relentless sun will take it. Perhaps the desert will turn the place back into the space. Perhaps human efforts will be nothing in comparison to the environment that Knight chose to inhabit, the one that early explorers called the Valley of the Dead.

Jo Hernandez, director of SPACES (an organization that helped safeguard Watts Towers and other works of outsider art) suggests that there is not much hope for Salvation Mountain because "it's out in the middle of the desert and with the way it is formed and the kind of materials [Knight] uses, I just don't see any possibility that in the end, it will be able to be 'saved.'" Without that hope, the current attempts to preserve, to gather funds that might bankroll preservation, are but a drop in the bucket compared to the rolling tide of the desert. Without Knight's daily upkeep driven by his sense of calling, Salvation Mountain may simply fall away. Hernandez maintains that "it's an ephemeral piece and hopefully we can let it die gracefully. I hate to say that, but I'm just trying to be realistic."[43]

And so Salvation Mountain continues to have stories told about it—both its life and its dying. Each one represents a distinct interpretation of the symbols, each one offers a different vision of the future, and each one makes its own claim to authority and authenticity. It was storytelling that first made Salvation Mountain a *place,* and stories about it continue in abundance. Salvation Mountain will remain as long as there are those willing to tell its stories. Silence, then, appears to be the mountain's biggest enemy. Silence and the desert. The desert is the place to which Knight fled to create his own map of the world and its future. And it is the desert that attempts to reclaim the space, mechanically working to return it to what it once was, the middle of nowhere.

Notes

INTRODUCTION

1. Dan Westfall, Facebook post, February 11, 2014.

2. Leonard Knight, interview by author, June 2009, transcript in author's possession; Larry Yust, *Salvation Mountain: The Art of Leonard Knight* (Los Angeles: New Leaf Press, 1998), 3–30; Robert L. Pincus, "Mountain Man," *San Diego Union-Tribune*, May 1, 2005.

3. Knight, interview, June 2009.

4. Yust, *Salvation Mountain*, 21.

5. Knight, interview, June 2009.

6. Yust, *Salvation Mountain*, 25.

7. Knight, interview, June 2009.

8. Throughout this work I've replicated the messages as they are painted on the mountain rather than standardizing capitalization or punctuation.

9. Yust, *Salvation Mountain*, 29.

10. Mindy Munro, e-mail to author, July 15, 2011.

11. Yust, *Salvation Mountain*, 72.

12. Timothy Beal, *Roadside Religion: In Search of the Sacred, the Strange, and the Substance of Faith* (Boston: Beacon, 2005), 6.

13. David Morgan, *The Sacred Gaze: Religious Visual Culture in Theory and Practice* (Berkeley and Los Angeles: University of California Press, 2005), 9.

14. Sally M. Promey, "The Public Display of Religion," in *The Visual Culture of American Religions,* ed. David Morgan and Sally M. Promey (Berkeley and Los Angeles: University of California Press, 2001), 28.

CHAPTER 1

1. Gary Alan Fine, *Everyday Genius: Self-Taught Art and the Culture of Authenticity* (Chicago: University of Chicago Press, 2004), 25; and John Beardsley, "Imagining the Outsider," in *Vernacular Visionaries: International*

Outsider Art, ed. Annie Carlano (New Haven: Yale University Press, 2003), 11–15.

2.   John Maizels, *Raw Creation: Outsider Art and Beyond* (London: Phaidon Press, 1996), 114. See also Carlano, ed., *Vernacular Visionaries.* For a response that troubles the category of outsider art, see Beardsley, "Imagining the Outsider."

3.   Greg Bottoms, *The Colorful Apocalypse: Journey in Outsider Art* (Chicago: University of Chicago Press, 2007), 9.

4.   Fine, *Everyday Genius,* 4.

5.   Bottoms, *Colorful Apocalypse,* 11.

6.   John Beardsley, *Gardens of Revelation: Environments by Visionary Artists* (New York: Abbeville Press, 1995), 27.

7.   Knight, interview, June 2009

8.   Qtd. in Larry Yust, "The Interactive Mountain of Leonard Knight," Folk Art Society of America, http://www.folkart.org/mag/salva/salva.html, accessed June 1, 2009.

9.   Knight, interview, June 2009.

10.   Ibid.

11.   I want to thank the scholars who participated in the Center for the Study of Religion in American Culture's Bible in American Life Conference for helping me think through these issues. In particular, I want to thank James Bielo for helping me consider the creativity and imaginative space that can still be found in biblical literalism. James Bielo, "Literalism as Creativity: The Making of a Biblical Theme Park," Bible in American Life Conference, Indianapolis, August 6–8, 2014.

12.   Text on Salvation Mountain (italics added).

13.   Knight, interview, June 2009.

14.   Qtd. in Yust, *Salvation Mountain,* 79.

15.   Randall Balmer, *The Making of Evangelicalism: From Revivalism to Politics and Beyond* (Waco, TX: Baylor University Press, 2010), 29.

16.   Ibid., 32.

17.   Paul S. Boyer, *When Time Shall Be No More: Prophecy Belief in Modern American Culture* (Cambridge, MA: Belknap Press, 1994), 317.

18.   Thomas W. Overholt, *Channels of Prophecy: The Social Dynamics of Prophetic Activity* (Eugene, OR: Wipf and Stock, 1989), 1, 24.

19.   Ibid., 70.

20. Ibid., 71, 35.

21. Aaron Huey, "Remembering a Folk Art Visionary," National Geographic, http://proof.nationalgeographic.com/2014/02/14/remembering -a-folk-art-visionary, accessed March 10, 2014.

22. Beal, *Roadside Religion*, 6–11.

23. Thomas Merton, introduction to *The Wisdom of the Desert: Sayings from the Desert Fathers of the Fourth Century* (New York: New Directions Books, 1960), 5–6, 11. See also the preface and foreword to *The Sayings of the Desert Fathers*, trans. and with a foreword by Benedicta Ward (Kalamazoo, MI: Cistercian Publications, 1975).

24. Marilyn Dunn, *The Emergence of Monasticism: From the Desert Fathers to the Early Middle Ages* (Oxford: Blackwell, 2000), 19–20.

25. See Richard Rodriguez, *Darling: A Spiritual Autobiography* (New York: Viking, 2013), 29, 35, 49–51; and Paul Shepard, *Man and the Landscape* (Athens: University of Georgia Press, 2002) for more extended discussions of how the desert functions in this way.

26. Philip Sheldrake, *Spaces for the Sacred: Place, Memory, and Identity* (Baltimore: Johns Hopkins University Press, 2001), 91–94.

27. Jared Farmer, *On Zion's Mount: Mormons, Indians, and the American Landscape* (Cambridge, MA: Harvard University Press, 2008), 143.

28. Qtd. in Yust, *Salvation Mountain*, 83.

29. Knight, interview, June 2009.

30. There is a theoretical assumption about sacred space made in this work. That assumption is that sacred space, rather than being a point of sacred irruption as Mircea Eliade suggested many decades ago, is instead a cultural interpretation and production reinforced by ritual action. Sacred space is situational in that it requires the consent of the group who chooses to interpret the land in a symbolic fashion and often understands it as a point where divine and human stories merge. Belden Lane theorized sacred space best when he claimed that "above all else, sacred place is 'storied place'" (15). In this way, I am in agreement with the work of Jonathan Z. Smith, David Chidester, Edward Linenthal, and Belden Lane. For a discussion of these issues, see Mircea Eliade, *Patterns in Comparative Religion*, trans. Rosemary Sheed (New York: Meridian, 1958); Mircea Eliade, *The Sacred and the Profane: The Nature of Religion*, trans. Willard R. Trask (New York: Harvest, 1959); Jonathan Z. Smith, *Map Is Not Territory: Studies*

in the History of Religions (Chicago: University of Chicago Press, 1978); David Chidester and Edward T. Linenthal, eds., *American Sacred Space* (Bloomington: Indiana University Press, 1995); and Belden C. Lane, *Landscapes of the Sacred: Geography and Narrative in American Spirituality* (Baltimore: Johns Hopkins University Press, 2001).

31.   Knight, interview, June 2009.

32.   Chidester and Linenthal, *American Sacred Space*, 8–19. See also Yi-Fu Tuan, *Topophilia: A Study of Environmental Perception, Attitudes, and Values* (New York: Columbia University Press, 1974).

33.   Smith, in his *Map Is Not Territory* (143), asserted that sacred space is created and reinforced through ritual action. Chidester and Linenthal, in *American Sacred Space*, expand on this concept of ritual creation of sacred space. They argue that "we can identify sacred space as ritual space, a location for formalized, repeatable symbolic performances" and that the "human body plays a crucial role in the ritual production of space" (9–10).

34.   Beal, *Roadside Religion*, 7.

35.   S. Brent Plate, *A History of Religion in 5½ Objects: Bringing the Spiritual to Its Senses* (Boston: Beacon Press, 2014), 10–13.

36.   Lane, *Landscapes of the Sacred*, 7, 4.

37.   Religion scholar Kevin Lewis O'Neill has argued that it is important for us to address this messiness of religion and refuse to accept the dualistic perspective that much scholarship has embraced. This dualistic perspective suggests that there are clearly defined boundaries between sacred and profane, local and global, here and there. O'Neill instead argues for the concept of thinking about "affective spaces," spaces and experiences that take "place before consciousness and before discourse" and address the embodied nature of experience. See Kevin Lewis O'Neill, "Beyond Broken: Affective Spaces and the Study of American Religion," *JAAR* 81 (December 2013): 1093–116.

CHAPTER 2

1.   Mary Bellardo, qtd. in William deBuys, *Salt Dreams: Land and Water in Low-Down California* (Albuquerque: University of New Mexico Press, 1999), xvii.

2.   Marc Reisner, *Cadillac Desert: The American West and Its Disappearing Water* (New York: Viking Press, 1986), 129.

3.   Kevin Starr, *Material Dreams: Southern California Through the 1920s* (New York: Oxford University Press, 1990), 25.

4.   Denise Moreno Ducheny, "Two Valleys, Two Nations—One River, One Region," in *Imperial-Mexicali Valleys: Development and Environment of the U.S.-Mexican Border Region,* ed. Kimberly Collins, Paul Ganster, Cheryl Mason, Eduardo Sanchez Lopez, and Margarito Quintero-Nunez (San Diego: San Diego State University Press, 2004), xi.

5.   Pat Laflin, "The Salton Sea: California's Overlooked Treasure," Coachella Valley Historical Society, *Periscope* 4 (1995). The flooding of the river and the changing of its course have been estimated to be somewhere between every twenty and fifty years before dams started changing the course of the Colorado River.

6.   Reisner, *Cadillac Desert,* 4.

7.   Ibid., 129.

8.   Starr, *Material Dreams,* 7.

9.   *Plagues and Pleasures of the Salton Sea,* DVD, Tilapia Films, 2007.

10.   Reisner, *Cadillac Desert,* 130.

11.   Robert Sperry, "When the Imperial Valley Fought for Its Life," *Journal of San Diego History* 21 (Winter 1975). See http://www.sandiego history.org, accessed June 2014.

12.   deBuys, *Salt Dreams,* 7.

13.   U.S. Water News, http://www.uswaternews.com/archives/arcrights/ 7sandie4.html, accessed June 15, 2011.

14.   San Diego County Water Authority, "Water Authority—Imperial Irrigation District Water Transfer," http://www.sdcwa.org/water-transfer, accessed June 15, 2011.

15.   Gig Conaughton, "County-Imperial Water Transfer Dispute Heads to Arbitration," *San Diego Union Tribune,* March 18, 2007, http://www.nctimes. com/news/local/article_807d4744-530c-511c-ab48-0f9eec8088c6.html, accessed June 15, 2011.

16.   Laflin, "Salton Sea."

17.   *Plagues and Pleasures of the Salton Sea.*

18.   Sonny Bono Salton Sea National Wildlife Refuge, http://www.fws. gov/saltonsea, accessed June 12, 2011.

19.   *Plagues and Pleasures of the Salton Sea.*

20.   Nathan Onderdonk, Adriano Mazzini, Luke Shafer, and Henrik

Svensen, "Controls on the Geomorphic Expression and Evolution of Gryphons, Pools, and Caldera Features at Hydrothermal Seeps in the Salton Sea Geothermal Field, Southern California," http://www.csulb.edu/~nonderdo/Publications_files/Onderdonk2011.pdf, accessed June 11, 2011.

21. Kimberly Collins, "The Imperial Valley and Mexicali: An Introduction to the Region and Its People," in *Imperial-Mexicali Valleys*, 7–8.

22. Cheryl Mason, "Imperial County Employment Profile," in *Imperial-Mexicali Valleys*, 155.

23. James Gerber, "Explaining Low Income and High Unemployment in Imperial County," in *Imperial-Mexicali Valleys*, 99–100.

24. Mason, "Imperial County Employment Profile," 157.

25. Marcia Isabel Campillo Lopez, "Transborder Public Art: Murals and Graffiti in the Imperial-Mexicali Valley," in *Imperial-Mexicali Valleys*, 429.

26. Charlie LeDuff, "Parked in Desert, Waiting Out the Winter of Life," *New York Times*, December 17, 2004, http://www.nytimes.com/2004/12/17/national/17slab.html, accessed June 12, 2011.

27. Container Charlie's website, http://chaster.us, accessed June 12, 2011.

28. "East Jesus, Pop. 1, Elev. 75," pictureRoute66.com, December 1, 2009, http://pictureroute66.com/2009/12/01/east-jesus-pop-1-elev-75/, accessed June 12, 2011.

29. Huell Howser, *California's Gold #806—Slab City*, video, Huell Howser Productions, n.d.

30. Munro, e-mail to author, July 15, 2011.

31. Navy Seal Museum, http://www.navysealmuseum.com/heritage/training_stt.php, accessed June 8, 2011.

32. Commander, Navy Installations Command, "Welcome to Naval Air Facility El Centro," http://www.cnic.navy.mil/elcentro/index.htm, accessed June 12, 2011.

33. GlobalSecurity.org, "Naval Air Facility El Centro," http://www.globalsecurity.org/military/facility/el-centro.htm, accessed June 12, 2011.

34. California Department of Corrections and Rehabilitation, "Monthly Report of Population as of Midnight September 30, 2007," http://www.cdcr.ca.gov/Reports_Research/Offender_Information_Services_Branch/Monthly/TPOP1A/TPOP1Ad0709.pdf, accessed June 11.

35. Laws.com, "Calipatria State Prison," http://prison.laws.com/state-prison/california-state-prison/calipatria-state-prison, accessed June 11, 2011.

36. Sidney Weintraub, *Unequal Partners: The United States and Mexico* (Pittsburgh, PA: University of Pittsburgh Press, 2010), 116.

37. Joseph Nevins, *Operation Gatekeeper and Beyond: The War on "Illegals" and the Remaking of the U.S.-Mexico Boundary* (New York: Routledge, 2010), 3.

38. Weintraub, *Unequal Partners*, 102.

39. Department of Justice, Office of the Inspector General, "Background to the Office of the Inspector General Investigation," http://www.justice.gov/oig/special/9807/gkp01.htm, accessed June 17, 2011.

40. Nevins, *Operation Gatekeeper*, 105.

41. Ibid., 6.

42. William T. Vollmann, *Imperial* (New York: Viking Press, 2009), 943.

43. Weintraub, *Unequal Partners*, 116–17.

44. Vollmann, *Imperial*, 945.

45. Ibid., 1033–34.

CHAPTER 3

1. Yust, "Interactive Mountain of Leonard Knight."

2. Matthew 20:16 and Psalms 118:22.

3. Smith, *Map Is Not Territory*, 291.

4. Ibid.

5. Ibid., 292.

6. Bret E. Carroll, "Worlds in Space: American Religious Pluralism in Geographic Perspective," *Journal of the American Academy of Religion* 80, no. 2 (2012): 304–64.

7. Qtd. in ibid., 311.

8. Ibid., 312.

9. Tim Cresswell, *Place: A Short Introduction* (Oxford: Blackwell, 2004), 102–3.

10. Lewis Hyde, *The Gift: Creativity and the Artist in the Modern World* (New York: Vintage Books, 2007), xvi.

11. Ibid.

12. Ibid., xvii.

13. Ibid., xviii.

14. This was the fifth anonymous interview conducted on June 6, 2011. All further notes about similar anonymous interviews will appear this way:

Person 5 [the number varying according to the interviewee], interview,
June 6, 2011.

15. Knight, interview, June 2009.

16. Person 11, interview, July 27, 2010.

17. Knight, interview, June 2009.

18. Ibid.

19. Hyde, *Gift*, 2.

20. Sheila Seiler Lagrand, "Faith Made a Mountain, Part Two,"
Godspotting with Sheila, http://sheilalagrand.com/2010/10/faith-made-a
-mountain-part-two.html, accessed July 24, 2011.

21. Psalms 4:7–8 (NLT).

22. Karen Sykes, *Arguing with Anthropology: An Introduction to Critical
Theories of the Gift* (London: Routledge, 2005), 2–3, 59–60.

23. Ibid., 59.

24. Knight, interview, June 2009.

25. Brady Morlock, Facebook post, March 16, 2012.

26. Person 5, interview, July 26, 2010; Person 7, interview, July 26, 2010.

27. Person 10, interview, July 26, 2010; Person 19, interview, July 27, 2010;
Person 5, interview, July 26, 2010.

28. Person 20, interview, June 7, 2011; Person 39, interview, June 9, 2011.

29. Person 13, interview, June 7, 2011.

30. J. B. Jackson, *Landscape in Sight: Looking at America* (New Haven,
CT: Yale University Press, 1997), 309.

31. Hyde, *Gift*, 167.

32. Ibid., 195.

33. Kevin Eubank, personal communication, June 2011, in author's
possession.

34. Kevin Eubank, blog entry, January 26, 2011, http://kevinatlarge.com/
blog, accessed July 12, 2011.

35. Eubank, personal communication, June 2011.

36. Ibid.

37. Ibid.

38. Eubank, blog entry.

39. Stephen Prothero, *American Jesus: How the Son of God Became a
National Icon* (New York: Farrar, Straus and Giroux, 2003), 124–27.

40. Ibid., 130–31.

41. Ibid., 139.

42. Ibid., 141.

43. Mike Phippen, personal communication, June 2011, in author's possession.

44. Ibid.

45. Ibid.

46. Ibid.

47. Ibid.

48. Knight, interview, June 2009.

CHAPTER 4

1. Jon Krakauer, *Into the Wild* (New York: Anchor Books, 1996), author's note.

2. Penguin Random House, *Under the Banner of Heaven* page, http://www.randomhouse.com/features/krakauer/author.html, accessed June 25, 2012.

3. "Interview: Sean Penn," September 19, 2007, IGN, http://movies.ign.com/articles/821/821195p1.html, accessed December 31, 2010.

4. World Socialist website, http://www.wsws.org/articles/2007/oct2007/penn-o17.shtml, accessed December 31, 2010.

5. IMDb, http://www.imdb.com, *Into the Wild*, December 30, 2010. The $18.5 million gross estimate was made on March 23, 2008.

6. Krakauer, *Into the Wild*, author's note.

7. Ibid.

8. Ibid., 3.

9. Ibid., 29.

10. Ibid., 6, 7.

11. Ibid., 23.

12. Qtd. in Krakauer, *Into the Wild*, 15.

13. Ibid., 48.

14. Ibid., 51–52.

15. Ibid., 57.

16. *Christopher McCandless, Back to the Wild: The Photographs and Writings of Christopher McCandless* (St. George, UT: Twin Star Press, 2011), 136–37.

17. Krakauer, *Into the Wild*, 58.

18. Ibid., 32.

19. Ibid., 66.

20. Ibid., 163.

21. Ibid., 43.

22. *Into the Wild,* dir. Sean Penn, Square 1 Productions, DVD, 2008.

23. Krakauer, *Into the Wild,* 189.

CHAPTER 5

1. John 20:25 (NRSV).

2. David Morgan, *Religion and Material Culture: The Matter of Belief* (New York: Routledge, 2009), 7–11.

3. Ibid., 11.

4. David Morgan, *The Embodied Eye: Religious Visual Culture and the Social Life of Feeling* (Berkeley and Los Angeles: University of California Press, 2012), xvii–xix, 6.

5. Morgan, *Embodied Eye,* 55.

6. Ibid., 111, 166.

7. Douglas E. Cowan, "Online U-Topia: Cyberspace and the Mythology of Placelessness," *Journal for the Scientific Study of Religion* 44, no. 3 (2005): 257–63.

8. Ibid., 260.

9. Ibid., 261.

10. David Morgan, *The Lure of Images: A History of Religion and Visual Media in America* (New York: Routledge, 2007), 2.

11. Brian Annett, e-mail to author, June 19, 2011.

12. Diana Sainz, "Salvation Mountain—A Unique Surprise," *Diana Sainz—Through the Canon,* http://dianasainz.wordpress.com/2010/02/16/salvationmountain, accessed July 24, 2011.

13. Vollmann, *Imperial,* 1033.

14. Morgan, *Embodied Eye,* 160.

15. Beal, *Roadside Religion,* 114.

16. Ibid., 11.

17. Ibid.

18. Person 46, interview, June 6, 2011.

19. Person 13, interview, July 27, 2010.

20. David Morgan, *Visual Piety: A History and Theory of Popular*

Religious Images (Berkeley and Los Angeles: University of California Press, 1999).

21. Morgan, *Embodied Eye*, 33.

22. Morgan, *Religion in Material Culture*, 70–72.

23. Ibid., 59–70.

24. Person 19, interview, June 7, 2011.

25. Morgan has an interesting discussion of sensory hierarchies and the way that they might support particular ideologies. See Morgan, *Embodied Eye*, 161–65.

26. Munro, e-mail to author, July 15, 2011.

27. David Chidester, *Authentic Fakes: Religion and American Popular Culture* (Berkeley and Los Angeles: University of California Press, 2005), 72–73.

28. Sainz, "Salvation Mountain—A Unique Surprise."

29. Turner and Turner, *Image and Pilgrimage in Christian Culture*, 7–8, 30.

30. Simon Coleman and John Eade, "Introduction: Reframing Pilgrimage," in *Reframing Pilgrimage: Cultures in Motion*, ed. Simon Coleman and John Eade (New York: Routledge, 2004), 3–4. See also Simon Coleman and John Elsner, *Pilgrimage: Past and Present in the World Religions* (Cambridge: Harvard University Press, 1995), 199–202.

31. Coleman and Elsner, *Pilgrimage*, 208–14; John Eade and Michael J. Sallnow, "Introduction," in *Contesting the Sacred: The Anthropology of Christian Pilgrimage*, ed. John Eade and Michael Sallnow (London: Routledge, 1991).

32. Coleman and Elsner, *Pilgrimage*, 213.

33. Paul Elie, *The Life You Save May Be Your Own: An American Pilgrimage* (New York: Farrar, Straus and Giroux, 2003), x.

34. Lawrence A. Hoffman, *Meeting House Essays: Sacred Places and the Pilgrimage of Life* (Chicago: Liturgy Training Publications, 1991), 17–18.

35. Person 20, interview, June 7, 2011.

36. Person 2, interview, June 6, 2011.

37. Person 28, interview, July 28, 2010.

38. Person 33, interview, June 8, 2011; Person 26, interview, June 8, 2011.

39. Elie, *Life You Save May Be Your Own*, x.

40. Clara Hung, e-mail to author, July 17, 2011.

41. Cindy Holleman, e-mail to author, July 14, 2011.

42. Patrick Rea, e-mail to author, July 11, 2011.

CHAPTER 6

1.   Sue Grafton, *G Is for Gumshoe* (New York: Henry Holt, 1990), 2, 31.

2.   Marita Sturken and Lisa Cartwright, *Practices of Looking: An Introduction to Visual Culture* (New York: Oxford University Press, 2001), 48.

3.   Ibid., 48–49.

4.   Chidester and Linenthal, *American Sacred Space*, 18–19.

5.   Tony Perry, "Slab City Showdown—Artwork May Be Bulldozed as an Environmental Hazard," *Los Angeles Times,* July 11, 1994.

6.   PBS, Off the Map, "Salvation Mountain, Niland, California," http://www.pbs.org/independentlens/offthemap/html/travelogue_artist_10.htm, accessed June 1, 2009.

7.   Larry Bickman, "Desert Artist's Work," *Los Angeles Times,* April 17, 2002, B12.

8.   Perry, "Slab City Showdown."

9.   Pincus, "Mountain Man."

10.   Senator Barbara Boxer, qtd. in ibid.

11.   Knight, interview, June 2009.

12.   Ibid.

13.   Qtd. in Pincus, "Mountain Man."

14.   For a discussion of similar processes, see Kenneth E. Foote, *Shadowed Ground: America's Landscapes of Violence and Tragedy* (Austin: University of Texas Press, 1997), 8, 262–63.

15.   Colleen McDannell, *Material Christianity: Religion and Popular Culture in America* (New Haven, CT: Yale University Press, 1995), 163–65.

16.   Ibid., 165–66.

17.   Gillo Dorfles, "Kitsch," in *Kitsch: The World of Bad Taste,* ed. Gillo Dorfles (New York: Bell Publishing, 1975), 35.

18.   Harmann Brock, "Notes on the Problem of Kitsch," in *Kitsch,* 75.

19.   Gillo Dorfles, "Religious Trappings," in *Kitsch,* 141.

20.   Karl Pawek, "Christian Kitsch," in *Kitsch,* 143.

21.   Robert C. Solomon, "On Kitsch and Sentimentality," in *In Defense of Sentimentality,* by Robert C. Solomon (New York: Oxford University Press, 2004), 1.

22.   Ibid., 5–12, italics in the original.

23.   Beal, *Roadside Religion,* 157–58.

24. Solomon, "On Kitsch," 1.

25. Ibid., 3.

26. Exodus 20:4 and Deuteronomy 5:8.

27. Morgan, *Visual Piety*, 182.

28. McDannell, *Material Christianity*, 8.

29. Ann Taves, *Fits, Trances, and Visions: Experiencing Religion and Explaining Experience from Wesley to James* (Princeton: Princeton University Press, 1999), 46.

30. Greg Bishop, Joe Esterle, and Mike Marinacci, *Weird California* (New York: Sterling, 2006), 122.

31. Ibid., 124, 126.

32. Person 27, interview, July 28, 2010.

33. Person 11, interview, July 27, 2010; Person 5, interview, July 27, 2010.

34. TripAdvisor.com, reviews of Salvation Mountain, http://www.tripadvisor.com, accessed December 16, 2014.

35. Person 4, interview, July 27, 2010.

36. Person 21, interview, July 28, 2010.

37. Person 14, interview, July 24, 2010.

38. TripAdvisor.com, reviews of Salvation Mountain.

39. Person 14, interview, July 27, 2010.

40. Person 11, interview, July 27, 2010.

CHAPTER 7

1. See http://www.salvationmountaininc.org, accessed June 15, 2015.

2. Facebook post from Salvation Mountain Inc. to Salvation Mountain page, accessed May 9, 2013.

3. David Chidester and Edward T. Linenthal, "Introduction," in Chidester and Linenthal, *American Sacred Space*, 9.

4. Ibid., 15–18.

5. Peter W. Williams, "Sacred Space in North America," *Journal of the American Academy of Religion* 70, no. 3 (September 2002): 607.

6. Chidester and Linenthal, *American Sacred Space*, 18.

7. Kent Walker, interview with author, Salvation Mountain, June 30, 2012.

8. Ibid.

9. Ibid.

10. Overholt, *Channels of Prophecy*, 1.

11. Bob Makin, "Chatting with Third Day's Tai Anderson," MyCentralJersey.com, September 11, 2008, http://www.mycentraljersey.com/article/20080912/ENTERTAINMENT/80911160/Chatting-Third-Day-s-Tai-Anderson, accessed March 4, 2011.

12. John DiBiase, interview with Tai Anderson, January 2, 2008, http://www.jesusfreakhideout.com/interviews/thirdday2009.asp, accessed March 4, 2011.

13. Morgan, *Visual Piety*, 13.

14. Tona J. Hangen, *Redeeming the Dial: Radio, Religion and Popular Culture in America* (Chapel Hill: University of North Carolina Press, 2002), 17.

15. Andrew Beaujon, *Body Piercing Saved My Life: Inside the Phenomenon of Christian Rock* (Cambridge, MA: Da Capo Press, 2006), 6.

16. Heather Hendershot, *Shaking the World for Jesus: Median and Conservative Evangelical Culture* (Chicago: University of Chicago Press, 2004), 12, 20.

17. Ibid., 30.

18. Beaujon, *Body Piercing Saved My Life*, 6.

19. Third Day's website, http://www.thirdday.com, accessed February 28, 2011.

20. Hendershot, *Shaking the World for Jesus*, 59.

21. Qtd. in Beaujon, *Body Piercing Saved My Life*, 172, 178.

22. Cover of Third Day's CD *Revelation*, Sony Music, 2008.

23. DiBiase, interview with Tai Anderson.

24. Makin, "Chatting with Third Day's Tai Anderson."

25. Ibid.

26. See http://www.flixya.com/blog/1787716/Revelation, accessed March 4, 2011.

27. DiBiase, interview with Tai Anderson.

28. Third Day, *Revelation*, Sony Music, 2008, compact disc.

29. Nigel James with Third Day, *Lessons from the Road* (Colorado Springs, CO: Authentic, 2007), 22–23, 123.

30. *Live Revelations*, DVD, BMG, Brentwood, CA, 2009.

31. Angela Carone, "The Future of Salvation Mountain Uncertain," December 20, 2011, KPBS, http://www.kpbs.org/news/2011/dec/20/future-salvation-mountain-uncertain, accessed May 9, 2013.

32. See Erik Eckholm, "Talk of a Sale Fills a Hippie Haven with Bad Vibes," *New York Times*, March 11, 2015, http://www.nytimes.com/2015/03/12/us/talk-of-land-sale-divides-southern-californias-slab-city-dwellers.html, accessed June 15, 2015.

33. Bishop, Esterle, and Marinacci, *Weird California*, 122–26.

34. Beal, *Roadside Religion*, 11.

35. Person 48, interview, June 9, 2011.

36. Person 1, interview, June 6, 2011.

37. Ibid.

38. Coldwater Jane website, http://www.coldwaterjane.com/bad.aspx, accessed March 4, 2011.

39. Jill Sheets, "Chit Chatting with Coldwater Jane," Relatemag.com, July 7, 2010, http://www.relatemag.com/2010/07/singing-and-songwriting-duo-coldwater-jane, accessed March 4, 2011.

40. Coldwater Jane website, http://www.coldwaterjane.com/band.aspx, accessed July 5, 2011.

41. Kylie Campion, YouTube post, "Salvation Mountain (Slab City)," Leonard Knight's memorial service, March 15, 2013, posted by Ralph Guest, accessed March 21, 2014.

42. Tom C. Wang, Facebook post, February 2014, accessed March 14, 2014.

43. Jo Hernandez qtd. in Carone, "Future of Salvation Mountain Uncertain."

Index

Page numbers in italic text indicate illustrations.